Meet Mr. Mulliner

P. G. Wodehouse

Alpha Editions

This edition published in 2020

ISBN : 9789354034534

Design and Setting By
Alpha Editions
email - alphaedis@gmail.com

MEET
MR. MULLINER

BY
P. G. WODEHOUSE

HERBERT JENKINS LIMITED
3 YORK STREET ST. JAMES'S
LONDON S.W.1 ❀ ❀ ❀

TO THE
EARL OF OXFORD AND ASQUITH

CONTENTS

MEET MR. MULLINER

I

THE TRUTH ABOUT GEORGE

TWO men were sitting in the bar-parlour of the Angler's Rest as I entered it; and one of them, I gathered from his low, excited voice and wide gestures, was telling the other a story. I could hear nothing but an occasional " Biggest I ever saw in my life ! " and " Fully as large as that ! " but in such a place it was not difficult to imagine the rest; and when the second man, catching my eye, winked at me with a sort of humorous misery, I smiled sympathetically back at him.

The action had the effect of establishing a bond between us; and when the story-teller finished his tale and left, he came over to my table as if answering a formal invitation.

"Dreadful liars some men are," he said genially.

"Fishermen," I suggested, "are traditionally careless of the truth."

"He wasn't a fisherman," said my companion. "That was our local doctor. He was telling me about his latest case of dropsy. Besides"—he tapped me earnestly on the knee—"you must not fall into the popular error about fishermen. Tradition has maligned them. I am a fisherman myself, and I have never told a lie in my life."

I could well believe it. He was a short, stout, comfortable man of middle age, and the thing that struck me first about him was the extraordinarily childlike candour of his eyes. They were large and round and honest. I would have bought oil stock from him without a tremor.

The door leading into the white dusty road opened, and a small man with rimless pince-nez and an anxious expression shot in like a rabbit and had consumed a gin and ginger-beer almost before we knew he was there. Having thus refreshed himself, he stood looking at us, seemingly ill at ease.

"N-n-n-n-n-n——" he said.

We looked at him inquiringly.

" N-n-n-n-n-n-ice d-d-d-d———"

His nerve appeared to fail him, and he vanished as abruptly as he had come.

" I think he was leading up to telling us that it was a nice day," hazarded my companion.

" It must be very embarrassing," I said, " for a man with such a painful impediment in his speech to open conversation with strangers."

" Probably trying to cure himself. Like my nephew George. Have I ever told you about my nephew George ? "

I reminded him that we had only just met, and that this was the first time I had learned that he had a nephew George.

" Young George Mulliner. My name is Mulliner. I will tell you about George's case —in many ways a rather remarkable one."

My nephew George (said Mr. Mulliner) was as nice a young fellow as you would ever wish to meet, but from childhood up he had been cursed with a terrible stammer. If he had had to earn his living, he would undoubtedly have found this affliction a great handicap, but fortunately his father had left him a comfortable income ; and George spent a not unhappy life, residing in the village where he had been born and passing his days in the usual country sports and his evenings in doing cross-word puzzles. By the time he was thirty he knew more about Eli, the prophet, Ra, the Sun God, and the bird Emu than anybody else in the county except Susan Blake, the vicar's daughter, who had also taken up the solving of cross-word puzzles and was the first girl in Worcestershire to find out the meaning of " stearine " and " crepuscular."

It was his association with Miss Blake that first turned George's thoughts to a serious endeavour to cure himself of his stammer. Naturally, with this hobby in common, the young people saw a great deal of one another : for George was always looking in at the vicarage to ask her if she knew a word of seven letters meaning " appertaining to the profession of plumbing," and Susan was just as constant a caller at George's cosy little cottage—being frequently stumped, as girls will be, by words of eight letters signifying " largely used in the manufacture of poppet-valves." The consequence was that one evening, just after she had helped him out of a tight place with the word "disestablishmentarianism," the boy suddenly awoke to the truth and realised that she was all the world to him—or, as he put it to himself from force of habit, precious, beloved, darling, much-loved, highly esteemed or valued.

And yet, every time he tried to tell her so, he could get no farther than a sibilant gurgle which was no more practical use than a hiccup.

Something obviously had to be done, and George went to London to see a specialist.

" Yes ? " said the specialist.

" I-I-I-I-I-I-I—— " said George.

" You were saying—— ? "

" Woo-woo-woo-woo-woo-woo—— "

" Sing it," said the specialist.

" S-s-s-s-s-s-s-s—— ? " said George, puzzled.

The specialist explained. He was a kindly man with moth-eaten whiskers and an eye like a meditative cod-fish.

" Many people," he said, " who are unable to articulate clearly in ordinary speech find themselves lucid and bell-like when they burst into song.''

It seemed a good idea to George. He thought for a moment ; then threw his head back, shut his eyes, and let it go in a musical baritone.

'' I love a lassie, a bonny, bonny lassie,'' sang George. '' She's as pure as the lily in the dell.''

'' No doubt,'' said the specialist, wincing a little.

'' She's as sweet as the heather, the bonny purple heather—Susan, my Worcestershire bluebell.''

'' Ah ! '' said the specialist. '' Sounds a nice girl. Is this she ? '' he asked, adjusting his glasses and peering at the photograph which George had extracted from the interior of the left side of his under-vest.

George nodded, and drew in breath.

'' Yes, sir,'' he carolled, '' that's my baby. No, sir, don't mean maybe. Yes, sir, that's my baby now. And, by the way, by the way, when I meet that preacher I shall say— ' Yes, sir, that's my—— ' ''

'' Quite,'' said the specialist, hurriedly. He had a sensitive ear. '' Quite, quite.''

" If you knew Susie like I know Susie,"
George was beginning, but the other stopped
him.

" Quite. Exactly. I shouldn't wonder.
And now," said the specialist, " what precisely is the trouble ? No," he added,
hastily, as George inflated his lungs, " don't
sing it. Write the particulars on this piece
of paper."

George did so.

" H'm ! " said the specialist, examining
the screed. " You wish to woo, court, and
become betrothed, engaged, affianced to this
girl, but you find yourself unable, incapable,
incompetent, impotent, and powerless. Every
time you attempt it, your vocal cords fail,
fall short, are insufficient, wanting, deficient,
and go blooey."

George nodded.

" A not unusual case. I have had to deal
with this sort of thing before. The effect of
love on the vocal cords of even a normally
eloquent subject is frequently deleterious.
As regards the habitual stammerer, tests have
shown that in ninety-seven point five six
nine recurring of cases the divine passion
reduces him to a condition where he sounds

like a soda-water siphon trying to recite Gunga Din. There is only one cure."

" W-w-w-w-w——? " asked George.

" I will tell you. Stammering," proceeded the specialist, putting the tips of his fingers together and eyeing George benevolently, " is mainly mental and is caused by shyness, which is caused by the inferiority complex, which in its turn is caused by suppressed desires or introverted inhibitions or something. The advice I give to all young men who come in here behaving like soda-water siphons is to go out and make a point of speaking to at least three perfect strangers every day. Engage these strangers in conversation, persevering no matter how priceless a chump you may feel, and before many weeks are out you will find that the little daily dose has had its effect. Shyness will wear off, and with it the stammer."

And, having requested the young man— in a voice of the clearest timbre, free from all trace of impediment—to hand over a fee of five guineas, the specialist sent George out into the world.

The more George thought about the advice

he had been given, the less he liked it. He shivered in the cab that took him to the station to catch the train back to East Wobsley. Like all shy young men, he had never hitherto looked upon himself as shy— preferring to attribute his distaste for the society of his fellows to some subtle rareness of soul. But now that the thing had been put squarely up to him, he was compelled to realise that in all essentials he was a perfect rabbit. The thought of accosting perfect strangers and forcing his conversation upon them sickened him.

But no Mulliner has ever shirked an unpleasant duty. As he reached the platform and strode along it to the train, his teeth were set, his eyes shone with an almost fanatical light of determination, and he intended before his journey was over to conduct three heart-to-heart chats if he had to sing every bar of them.

The compartment into which he had made his way was empty at the moment, but just before the train started a very large, fierce-looking man got in. George would have preferred somebody a little less formidable for his first subject, but he braced himself and bent forward. And, as he did so, the man spoke.

" The wur-wur-wur-wur-weather," he said, " sus-sus-seems to be ter-ter-taking a tur-tur-turn for the ber-ber-better, der-doesn't it ? "

George sank back as if he had been hit between the eyes. The train had moved out of the dimness of the station by now, and the sun was shining brightly on the speaker, illuminating his knobbly shoulders, his craggy jaw, and, above all, the shockingly choleric look in his eyes. To reply " Y-y-y-y-y-y-y-yes " to such a man would obviously be madness.

But to abstain from speech did not seem to be much better as a policy. George's silence appeared to arouse this man's worst passions. His face had turned purple and he glared painfully.

" I uk-uk-asked you a sus-sus-civil quk-quk-quk," he said, irascibly. " Are you d-d-d-d-deaf ? "

All we Mulliners have been noted for our presence of mind. To open his mouth, point to his tonsils, and utter a strangled gurgle was with George the work of a moment.

The tension relaxed. The man's annoyance abated.

"D-d-d-dumb?" he said, commiseratingly. "I beg your p-p-p-p-pup. I t-t-trust I have not caused you p-p-p-p-pup. It m-must be tut-tut-tut-tut-tut not to be able to sus-sus-speak fuf-fuf-fuf-fuf-fluently."

He then buried himself in his paper, and George sank back in his corner, quivering in every limb.

To get to East Wobsley, as you doubtless know, you have to change at Ippleton and take the branch-line. By the time the train reached this junction, George's composure was somewhat restored. He deposited his belongings in a compartment of the East Wobsley train, which was waiting in a glued manner on the other side of the platform, and, finding that it would not start for some ten minutes, decided to pass the time by strolling up and down in the pleasant air.

It was a lovely afternoon. The sun was gilding the platform with its rays, and a gentle breeze blew from the west. A little brook ran tinkling at the side of the road; birds were singing in the hedgerows; and through the trees could be discerned dimly the noble façade of the County Lunatic Asylum. Soothed by his surroundings, George began to feel so refreshed that he regretted that in this wayside station there was no one present whom he could engage in talk.

It was at this moment that the distinguished-looking stranger entered the platform.

The new-comer was a man of imposing physique, simply dressed in pyjamas, brown boots, and a mackintosh. In his hand he carried a top-hat, and into this he was dipping his fingers, taking them out, and then waving them in a curious manner to right and left. He nodded so affably to George that the latter, though a little surprised at the other's costume, decided to speak. After all, he reflected, clothes do not make the man, and, judging from the other's smile, a warm heart appeared to beat beneath that orange-and-mauve striped pyjama jacket.

" N-n-n-n-nice weather," he said.

" Glad you like it," said the stranger. " I ordered it specially."

George was a little puzzled by this remark, but he persevered.

" M-might I ask wur-wur-what you are dud-doing ? "

" Doing ? "

" With that her-her-her-her-hat ? "

" Oh, with this hat ? I see what you mean. Just scattering largesse to the multitude," replied the stranger, dipping his fingers once more and waving them with a generous gesture. " Devil of a bore, but it's expected of a man in my position. The fact is," he said, linking his arm in George's and speaking in a confidential undertone, " I'm the Emperor of Abyssinia. That's my palace over there," he said, pointing through the trees. " Don't let it go any farther. It's not supposed to be generally known."

It was with a rather sickly smile that George now endeavoured to withdraw his arm from that of his companion, but the other would have none of this aloofness. He seemed to be in complete agreement with Shakespeare's dictum that a friend, when found, should be grappled to you with hooks of steel. He held George in a vice-like grip and drew him into a recess of the platform. He looked about him, and seemed satisfied.

" We are alone at last," he said.

This fact had already impressed itself with sickening clearness on the young man. There are few spots in the civilised world more deserted than the platform of a small country station. The sun shone on the smooth asphalt, on the gleaming rails, and on the machine which, in exchange for a penny placed in the slot marked " Matches," would supply a package of wholesome butter-scotch—but on nothing else.

What George could have done with at the moment was a posse of police armed with stout clubs, and there was not even a dog in sight.

" I've been wanting to talk to you for a long time," said the stranger, genially.

" Huh-huh-have you ? " said George.

" Yes. I want your opinion of human sacrifices."

George said he didn't like them.

" Why not ? " asked the other, surprised.

George said it was hard to explain. He just didn't.

" Well, I think you're wrong," said the Emperor. " I know there's a school of thought growing up that holds your views, but I disapprove of it. I hate all this modern advanced thought. Human sacrifices have always been good enough for the Emperors of Abyssinia, and they're good enough for me. Kindly step in here, if you please."

He indicated the lamp-and-mop room, at which they had now arrived. It was a dark and sinister apartment, smelling strongly of oil and porters, and was probably the last place on earth in which George would have wished to be closeted with a man of such peculiar views. He shrank back.

" You go in first," he said.

" No larks," said the other, suspiciously.

" L-l-l-l-larks ? "

" Yes. No pushing a fellow in and locking the door and squirting water at him through the window. I've had that happen to me before."

" Sus-certainly not."

" Right ! " said the Emperor. " You're a gentleman and I'm a gentleman. Both gentlemen. Have you a knife, by the way ? We shall need a knife."

" No. No knife."

" Ah, well," said the Emperor, " then we'll have to look about for something else. No doubt we shall manage somehow."

And with the debonair manner which so became him, he scattered another handful of largesse and walked into the lamp-room.

It was not the fact that he had given his word as a gentleman that kept George from locking the door. There is probably no family on earth more nicely scrupulous as regards keeping its promises than the Mulliners, but I am compelled to admit that, had George been able to find the key, he would have locked that door without hesitation. Not being able to find the key, he had to be satisfied with banging it. This done, he leaped back and raced away down the platform. A confused noise within seemed to indicate that the Emperor had become involved with some lamps.

George made the best of the respite. Covering the ground at a high rate of speed, he flung himself into the train and took refuge under the seat.

There he remained, quaking. At one time he thought that his uncongenial acquaintance had got upon his track, for the door of the compartment opened and a cool wind blew in upon him. Then, glancing along the floor, he perceived feminine ankles.

The relief was enormous, but even in his relief George, who was the soul of modesty, did not forget his manners. He closed his eyes.

A voice spoke.

" Porter ! "

" Yes, ma'am ? "

" What was all that disturbance as I came into the station ? "

" Patient escaped from the asylum, ma'am."

" Good gracious ! "

The voice would undoubtedly have spoken further, but at this moment the train began to move. There came the sound of a body descending upon a cushioned seat, and some little time later the rustling of a paper. The train gathered speed and jolted on.

George had never before travelled under the seat of a railway-carriage ; and, though he belonged to the younger generation, which is supposed to be so avid of new experiences, he had no desire to do so now. He decided to emerge, and, if possible, to emerge with the minimum of ostentation. Little as he knew of women, he was aware that as a sex they are apt to be startled by the sight of men crawling out from under the seats of compartments. He began his manœuvres by poking out his head and surveying the terrain.

All was well. The woman, in her seat across the way, was engrossed in her paper. Moving in a series of noiseless wriggles, George extricated himself from his hiding-place and, with a twist which would have been impossible to a man not in the habit of doing Swedish exercises daily before break-fast, heaved himself into the corner seat. The woman continued reading her paper.

The events of the past quarter of an hour had tended rather to drive from George's mind the mission which he had undertaken on leaving the specialist's office. But now, having leisure for reflection, he realised that, if he meant to complete his first day of the cure, he was allowing himself to run sadly behind schedule. Speak to three strangers, the specialist had told him, and up to the present he had spoken to only one. True, this one had been a pretty considerable stranger, and a less conscientious young man than George Mulliner might have considered himself justified in chalking him up on the score-board as one and a half or even two. But George had the dogged, honest Mulliner streak in him, and he refused to quibble.

He nerved himself for action, and cleared his throat.

" Ah-h'rm ! " said George.

And, having opened the ball, he smiled a winning smile and waited for his companion to make the next move.

The move which his companion made was in an upwards direction, and measured from six to eight inches. She dropped her paper and regarded George with a pale-eyed horror. One pictures her a little in the position of Robinson Crusoe when he saw the footprint in the sand. She had been convinced that she was completely alone, and lo ! out of space a voice had spoken to her. Her face worked, but she made no remark.

George, on his side, was also feeling a little ill at ease. Women always increased his natural shyness. He never knew what to say to them.

Then a happy thought struck him. He

had just glanced at his watch and found the hour to be nearly four-thirty. Women, he knew, loved a drop of tea at about this time, and fortunately there was in his suit-case a full thermos-flask.

" Pardon me, but I wonder if you would care for a cup of tea ? " was what he wanted to say, but, as so often happened with him when in the presence of the opposite sex, he could get no farther than a sort of sizzling sound like a cockroach calling to its young.

The woman continued to stare at him. Her eyes were now about the size of regulation standard golf-balls, and her breathing suggested the last stages of asthma. And it was at this point that George, struggling for speech, had one of those inspirations which frequently come to Mulliners. There flashed into his mind what the specialist had told him about singing. Say it with music— that was the thing to do.

He delayed no longer.

" Tea for two and two for tea and me for you and you for me—— "

He was shocked to observe his companion turning Nile-green. He decided to make his meaning clearer.

" I have a nice thermos. I have a full thermos. Won't you share my thermos, too ? When skies are grey and you feel you are blue, tea sends the sun smiling through. I have a nice thermos. I have a full thermos. May I pour out some for you ? "

You will agree with me, I think, that no invitation could have been more happily put, but his companion was not responsive. With one last agonised look at him, she closed her eyes and sank back in her seat. Her lips had now turned a curious grey-blue colour, and they were moving feebly. She reminded George, who, like myself, was a keen fisherman, of a newly-gaffed salmon.

George sat back in his corner, brooding. Rack his brain as he might, he could think of no topic which could be guaranteed to interest, elevate, and amuse. He looked out of the window with a sigh.

The train was now approaching the dear old familiar East Wobsley country. He began to recognise landmarks. A wave of sentiment poured over George as he thought of Susan, and he reached for the bag of buns which he had bought at the refreshment room at Ippleton. Sentiment always made him hungry.

He took his thermos out of the suit-case, and, unscrewing the top, poured himself out a cup of tea. Then, placing the thermos on the seat, he drank.

He looked across at his companion. Her eyes were still closed, and she uttered little sighing noises. George was half inclined to renew his offer of tea, but the only tune he could remember was " Hard-Hearted Hanna, the Vamp from Savannah," and it was difficult to fit suitable words to it. He ate his bun and gazed out at the familiar scenery.

Now, as you approach East Wobsley, the train, I must mention, has to pass over some points ; and so violent is the sudden jerking that strong men have been known to spill their beer. George, forgetting this in his preoccupation, had placed the thermos only a few inches from the edge of the seat. The result was that, as the train reached the points, the flask leaped like a live thing, dived to the floor, and exploded.

Even George was distinctly upset by the sudden sharpness of the report. His bun sprang from his hand and was dashed to

fragments.   He blinked thrice in rapid succession.   His heart tried to jump out of his
mouth and loosened a front tooth.

But on the woman opposite the effect of
the untoward occurrence was still more
marked.   With a single piercing shriek, she
rose from her seat straight into the air like
a rocketing pheasant ; and, having clutched
the communication-cord, fell back again.
Impressive as her previous leap had been,
she excelled it now by several inches.   I do
not know what the existing record for the
Sitting High-Jump is, but she undoubtedly
lowered it ; and if George had been a member
of the Olympic Games Selection Committee,
he would have signed this woman up immediately.

It is a curious thing that, in spite of the
railway companies' sporting willingness to
let their patrons have a tug at the extremely
moderate price of five pounds a go, very few
people have ever either pulled a communication-cord or seen one pulled.   There is, thus,
a widespread ignorance as to what precisely
happens on such occasions.

The procedure, George tells me, is as

follows : First there comes a grinding noise, as the brakes are applied. Then the train stops. And finally, from every point of the compass, a seething mob of interested on-lookers begins to appear.

It was about a mile and a half from East Wobsley that the affair had taken place, and as far as the eye could reach the country-side was totally devoid of humanity. A moment before nothing had been visible but smiling cornfields and broad pasture-lands ; but now from east, west, north, and south running figures began to appear. We must remember that George at the time was in a somewhat overwrought frame of mind, and his statements should therefore be accepted with caution ; but he tells me that out of the middle of a single empty meadow, entirely devoid of cover, no fewer than twenty-seven distinct rustics suddenly appeared, having undoubtedly shot up through the ground.

The rails, which had been completely unoccupied, were now thronged with so dense a crowd of navvies that it seemed to George absurd to pretend that there was any unemployment in England. Every member of the labouring classes throughout the

country was so palpably present. Moreover, the train, which at Ippleton had seemed
sparsely occupied, was disgorging passengers
from every door. It was the sort of mob-
scene which would have made David W.
Griffith scream with delight ; and it looked,
George says, like Guest Night at the Royal
Automobile Club. But, as I say, we must
remember that he was overwrought.

It is difficult to say what precisely would
have been the correct behaviour of your
polished man of the world in such a situation.
I think myself that a great deal of sang-froid
and address would be required even by the
most self-possessed in order to pass off such
a contretemps. To George, I may say at
once, the crisis revealed itself immediately
as one which he was totally incapable of
handling. The one clear thought that stood
out from the welter of his emotions was the
reflection that it was advisable to remove
himself, and to do so without delay. Drawing a deep breath, he shot swiftly off the mark.

All we Mulliners have been athletes ; and
George, when at the University, had been
noted for his speed of foot. He ran now as

B

he had never run before. His statement,
however, that as he sprinted across the first
field he distinctly saw a rabbit shoot an
envious glance at him as he passed and shrug
its shoulders hopelessly, I am inclined to
discount. George, as I have said before,
was a little over-excited.

Nevertheless, it is not to be questioned
that he made good going. And he had need
to, for after the first instant of surprise, which
had enabled him to secure a lead, the whole
mob was pouring across country after him ;
and dimly, as he ran, he could hear voices
in the throng informally discussing the
advisability of lynching him. Moreover, the
field through which he was running, a moment
before a bare expanse of green, was now black
with figures, headed by a man with a beard
who carried a pitchfork. George swerved
sharply to the right, casting a swift glance
over his shoulder at his pursuers. He disliked them all, but especially the man with
the pitchfork.

It is impossible for one who was not an
eye-witness to say how long the chase continued and how much ground was covered
by the interested parties. I know the East

Wobsley country well, and I have checked George's statements ; and, if it is true that he travelled east as far as Little-Wigmarsh-in-the-Dell and as far west as Higgleford-cum-Wortlebury-beneath-the-Hill, he must undoubtedly have done a lot of running.

But a point which must not be forgotten is that, to a man not in a condition to observe closely, the village of Higgleford-cum-Wortle-bury-beneath-the-Hill might easily not have been Higgleford - cum - Wortlebury - beneath-the-Hill at all, but another hamlet which in many respects closely resembles it. I need scarcely say that I allude to Lesser-Snods-bury-in-the-Vale.

Let us assume, therefore, that George, having touched Little-Wigmarsh-in-the-Dell, shot off at a tangent and reached Lesser-Snodsbury-in-the-Vale. This would be a considerable run. And, as he remembers flitting past Farmer Higgins's pigsty and the Dog and Duck at Pondlebury Parva and splashing through the brook Wipple at the point where it joins the River Wopple, we can safely assume that, wherever else he went, he got plenty of exercise.

But the pleasantest of functions must

end, and, just as the setting sun was gilding
the spire of the ivy-covered church of St.
Barnabas the Resilient, where George as a
child had sat so often, enlivening the tedium
of the sermon by making faces at the choir-
boys, a damp and bedraggled figure might
have been observed crawling painfully along
the High Street of East Wobsley in the
direction of the cosy little cottage known to
its builder as Chatsworth and to the village
tradesmen as "Mulliner's."

It was George, home from the hunting-
field.

Slowly George Mulliner made his way to
the familiar door, and, passing through it,
flung himself into his favourite chair. But
a moment later a more imperious need than
the desire to rest forced itself upon his attention. Rising stiffly, he tottered to the
kitchen and mixed himself a revivifying
whisky-and-soda. Then, refilling his glass,
he returned to the sitting-room, to find that
it was no longer empty. A slim, fair girl,
tastefully attired in tailor-made tweeds, was
leaning over the desk on which he kept his
Dictionary of English Synonyms.

She looked up as he entered, startled.

" Why, Mr. Mulliner ! " she exclaimed. " What has been happening ? Your clothes are torn, rent, ragged, tattered, and your hair is all dishevelled, untrimmed, hanging loose or negligently, at loose ends ! "

George smiled a wan smile.

" You are right," he said. " And, what is more, I am suffering from extreme fatigue, weariness, lassitude, exhaustion, prostration, and languor."

The girl gazed at him, a divine pity in her soft eyes.

" I'm so sorry," she murmured. " So very sorry, grieved, distressed, afflicted, pained, mortified, dejected, and upset."

George took her hand. Her sweet sympathy had effected the cure for which he had been seeking so long. Coming on top of the violent emotions through which he had been passing all day, it seemed to work on him like some healing spell, charm, or incantation. Suddenly, in a flash, he realised that he was no longer a stammerer. Had he wished at that moment to say, " Peter Piper picked a peck of pickled peppers," he could have done it without a second thought.

But he had better things to say than that.

" Miss Blake—Susan—Susie." He took her other hand in his. His voice rang out clear and unimpeded. It seemed to him incredible that he had ever yammered at this girl like an overheated steam-radiator. " It cannot have escaped your notice that I have long entertained towards you sentiments warmer and deeper than those of ordinary friendship. It is love, Susan, that has been animating my bosom. Love, first a tiny seed, has burgeoned in my heart till, blazing into flame, it has swept away on the crest of its wave my diffidence, my doubt, my fears, and my foreboding, and now, like the topmost topaz of some ancient tower, it cries to all the world in a voice of thunder : ' You are mine ! My mate ! Predestined to me since Time first began ! ' As the star guides the mariner when, battered by boiling billows, he hies him home to the haven of hope and happiness, so do you gleam upon me along life's rough road and seem to say, ' Have courage, George ! I am here ! ' Susan, I am not an eloquent man—I cannot speak fluently as I could wish—but these simple words which you have just heard come from the heart, from the unspotted heart of an English gentleman. Susan, I love you. Will you be my wife, married woman, matron, spouse, help-meet, consort, partner or better half ? "

" Oh, George ! " said Susan. " Yes, yea, ay, aye ! Decidedly, unquestionably, indubitably, incontrovertibly, and past all dispute ! "

He folded her in his arms. And, as he did so, there came from the street outside —faintly, as from a distance—the sound of feet and voices. George leaped to the window. Rounding the corner, just by the Cow and Wheelbarrow public-house, licensed to sell ales, wines, and spirits, was the man with the pitchfork, and behind him followed a vast crowd.

" My darling," said George.   " For purely personal and private reasons, into which I need not enter, I must now leave you. Will you join me later ? "

" I will follow you to the ends of the earth," replied Susan, passionately.

" It will not be necessary," said George. " I am only going down to the coal-cellar. I shall spend the next half-hour or so there.

If anybody calls and asks for me, perhaps you would not mind telling them that I am out."

" I will, I will," said Susan. " And, George, by the way. What I really came here for was to ask you if you knew a hyphenated word of nine letters, ending in k and signifying an implement employed in the pursuit of agriculture."

" Pitch-fork, sweetheart," said George. " But you may take it from me, as one who knows, that agriculture isn't the only thing it is used in pursuit of."

And since that day (concluded Mr. Mulliner) George, believe me or believe me not, has not had the slightest trace of an impediment in his speech. He is now the chosen orator at all political rallies for miles around ; and so offensively self-confident has his manner become that only last Friday he had his eye blacked by a hay-corn-and-feed merchant of the name of Stubbs. It just shows you, doesn't it ?

II

A SLICE OF LIFE

THE conversation in the bar-parlour of the Anglers' Rest had drifted round to the subject of the Arts : and somebody asked if that film-serial, " The Vicissitudes of Vera," which they were showing down at the Bijou Dream, was worth seeing.

" It's very good," said Miss Postlethwaite, our courteous and efficient barmaid, who is a prominent first-nighter. " It's about this mad professor who gets this girl into his toils and tries to turn her into a lobster."

" Tries to turn her into a lobster ? " echoed we, surprised.

" Yes, sir. Into *a* lobster. It seems he collected thousands and thousands of lobsters and mashed them up and boiled down the juice from their glands and was just going to inject it into this Vera Dalrymple's spinal column when Jack Frobisher broke into the house and stopped him."

" Why did he do that ? "

" Because he didn't want the girl he loved to be turned into a lobster."

" What we mean," said we, " is why did the professor want to turn the girl into a lobster ? "

" He had a grudge against her."

This seemed plausible, and we thought it over for a while. Then one of the company shook his head disapprovingly.

" I don't like stories like that," he said. " They aren't true to life."

" Pardon me, sir," said a voice. And we were aware of Mr. Mulliner in our midst.

" Excuse me interrupting what may be a private discussion," said Mr. Mulliner, " but I chanced to overhear the recent remarks, and you, sir, have opened up a subject on which I happen to hold strong views—to wit, the question of what is and what is not true to life. How can we, with our limited experience, answer that question ? For all we know, at this very moment hundreds of young women all over the country may be in the process of being turned into lobsters

Forgive my warmth, but I have suffered a good deal from this sceptical attitude of mind which is so prevalent nowadays. I have even met people who refused to believe my story about my brother Wilfred, purely because it was a little out of the ordinary run of the average man's experience."

Considerably moved, Mr. Mulliner ordered a hot Scotch with a slice of lemon.

" What happened to your brother Wilfred ? Was he turned into a lobster ? "

" No," said Mr. Mulliner, fixing his honest blue eyes on the speaker, " he was not. It would be perfectly easy for me to pretend that he was turned into a lobster ; but I have always made it a practice—and I always shall make it a practice—to speak nothing but the bare truth. My brother Wilfred simply had rather a curious adventure."

My brother Wilfred (said Mr. Mulliner) is the clever one of the family. Even as a boy he was always messing about with chemicals, and at the University he devoted his time entirely to research. The result was that while still quite a young man he had won an established reputation as the inventor of what are known to the trade as Mulliner's Magic Marvels—a general term embracing the Raven Gipsy Face-Cream, the Snow of the Mountains Lotion, and many other preparations, some designed exclusively for the toilet, others of a curative nature, intended to alleviate the many ills to which the flesh is heir.

Naturally, he was a very busy man : and it is to this absorption in his work that I attribute the fact that, though—like all the Mulliners—a man of striking personal charm, he had reached his thirty-first year without ever having been involved in an affair of the heart. I remember him telling me once that he simply had no time for girls.

But we all fall sooner or later, and these strong concentrated men harder than any. While taking a brief holiday one year at Cannes, he met a Miss Angela Purdue, who was staying at his hotel, and she bowled him over completely.

She was one of these jolly, outdoor girls ; and Wilfred had told me that what attracted him first about her was her wholesome, sunburned complexion. In fact, he told Miss Purdue the same thing when, shortly after he had proposed and been accepted, she asked him in her girlish way what it was that had first made him begin to love her.

"It's such a pity," said Miss Purdue, "that the sunburn fades so soon. I do wish I knew some way of keeping it."

Even in his moments of holiest emotion Wilfred never forgot that he was a business man.

"You should try Mulliner's Raven Gipsy Face-Cream," he said. "It comes in two sizes—the small (or half-crown) jar and the large jar at seven shillings and sixpence. The large jar contains three and a half times as much as the small jar. It is applied nightly with a small sponge before retiring to rest. Testimonials have been received from numerous members of the aristocracy and may be examined at the office by any bonâ-fide inquirer."

"Is it really good?"

"I invented it," said Wilfred, simply.

She looked at him adoringly.

"How clever you are! Any girl ought to be proud to marry you."

"Oh, well," said Wilfred, with a modest wave of his hand.

"All the same, my guardian is going to be terribly angry when I tell him we're engaged."

"Why?"

"I inherited the Purdue millions when my uncle died, you see, and my guardian has always wanted me to marry his son, Percy."

Wilfred kissed her fondly, and laughed a defiant laugh.

"Jer mong feesh der selar," he said lightly.

But, some days after his return to London, whither the girl had preceded him, he had occasion to recall her words. As he sat in his study, musing on a preparation to cure the pip in canaries, a card was brought to him.

"Sir Jasper ffinch-ffarrowmere, Bart.," he read. The name was strange to him.

"Show the gentleman in," he said. And presently there entered a very stout man with a broad, pink face. It was a face whose natural expression should, Wilfred felt, have been jovial, but at the moment it was grave.

"Sir Jasper Finch-Farrowmere?" said Wilfred.

" ffinch - ffarrowmere," corrected the visitor, his sensitive ear detecting the capital letters.

" Ah yes. You spell it with two small f's."

" Four small f's."

" And to what do I owe the honour——— "

" I am Angela Purdue's guardian."

" How do you do ? A whisky-and-soda ? "

" I thank you, no. I am a total abstainer. I found that alcohol had a tendency to increase my weight, so I gave it up. I have also given up butter, potatoes, soups of all kinds and——— However," he broke off, the fanatic gleam which comes into the eyes of all fat men who are describing their system of diet fading away, " this is not a social call, and I must not take up your time with idle talk. I have a message for you, Mr. Mulliner. From Angela."

" Bless her ! " said Wilfred. " Sir Jasper, I love that girl with a fervour which increases daily."

" Is that so ? " said the baronet. " Well, what I came to say was, it's all off."

" What ? "

" All off. She sent me to say that she had thought it over and wanted to break the engagement."

Wilfred's eyes narrowed. He had not forgotten what Angela had said about this man wanting her to marry his son. He gazed piercingly at his visitor, no longer deceived by the superficial geniality of his appearance. He had read too many detective stories where the fat, jolly, red-faced man turns out a fiend in human shape to be a ready victim to appearances.

" Indeed ? " he said, coldly. " I should prefer to have this information from Miss Purdue's own lips."

" She won't see you. But, anticipating this attitude on your part, I brought a letter from her. You recognise the writing ? "

Wilfred took the letter. Certainly, the hand was Angela's, and the meaning of the words he read unmistakable. Nevertheless, as he handed the missive back, there was a hard smile on his face.

" There is such a thing as writing a letter under compulsion," he said.

The baronet's pink face turned mauve.

" What do you mean, sir ? "

" What I say."

" Are you insinuating—— "

" Yes, I am."

" Pooh, sir ! "

" Pooh to you ! " said Wilfred. " And, if you want to know what I think, you poor ffish, I believe your name is spelled with a capital F, like anybody else's."

Stung to the quick, the baronet turned on his heel and left the room without another word.

Although he had given up his life to chemical research, Wilfred Mulliner was no mere dreamer. He could be the man of action when necessity demanded. Scarcely had his visitor left when he was on his way to the Senior Test-Tubes, the famous chemists' club in St. James's. There, consulting Kelly's " County Families," he learnt that Sir Jasper's address was ffinch Hall in Yorkshire. He had found out all he wanted to know. It was at ffinch Hall, he decided, that Angela must now be immured.

For that she was being immured somewhere he had no doubt. That letter, he was positive, had been written by her under stress of threats. The writing was Angela's, but he declined to believe that she was responsible for the phraseology and sentiments. He remembered reading a story where the heroine was forced into courses which she would not otherwise have contemplated by the fact that somebody was standing over her with a flask of vitriol. Possibly this was what that bounder of a baronet had done to Angela.

Considering this possibility, he did not blame her for what she had said about him, Wilfred, in the second paragraph of her note. Nor did he reproach her for signing herself " Yrs truly, A. Purdue." Naturally, when baronets are threatening to pour vitriol down her neck, a refined and sensitive young girl cannot pick her words. This sort of thing must of necessity interfere with the selection of the *mot juste*.

That afternoon, Wilfred was in a train on his way to Yorkshire. That evening, he was in the ffinch Arms in the village of which Sir Jasper was the squire. That night, he was in the gardens of ffinch Hall, prowling softly round the house, listening.

And presently, as he prowled, there came to his ears from an upper window a sound that made him stiffen like a statue and clench his hands till the knuckles stood out white under the strain.

It was the sound of a woman sobbing.

Wilfred spent a sleepless night, but by morning he had formed his plan of action. I will not weary you with a description of the slow and tedious steps by which he first made the acquaintance of Sir Jasper's valet, who was an habitué of the village inn, and then by careful stages won the man's confidence with friendly words and beer. Suffice it to say that, about a week later, Wilfred had induced this man with bribes to leave suddenly on the plea of an aunt's illness, supplying—so as to cause his employer no inconvenience—a cousin to take his place.

This cousin, as you will have guessed, was Wilfred himself. But a very different Wilfred from the dark-haired, clean-cut young scientist who had revolutionised the world of chemistry a few months before by proving that $H_2O+b3g4z7-m9z8=g6f5p3x$. Before leaving London on what he knew would be a dark and dangerous enterprise, Wilfred had taken the precaution of calling in at a well-

known costumier's and buying a red wig.
He had also purchased a pair of blue
spectacles : but for the *rôle* which he had
now undertaken these were, of course, use-
less. A blue-spectacled valet could not but
have aroused suspicion in the most guileless
baronet. All that Wilfred did, therefore, in
the way of preparation, was to don the wig,
shave off his moustache, and treat his face
to a light coating of the Raven Gipsy Face-
Cream. This done, he set out for ffinch Hall.

Externally, ffinch Hall was one of those
gloomy, sombre country-houses which seem
to exist only for the purpose of having
horrid crimes committed in them. Even in
his brief visit to the grounds, Wilfred had
noticed fully half a dozen places which
seemed incomplete without a cross indicating
spot where body was found by the police.
It was the sort of house where ravens croak
in the front garden just before the death of
the heir, and shrieks ring out from behind
barred windows in the night.

Nor was its interior more cheerful. And,
as for the personnel of the domestic staff,
that was less exhilarating than anything else
about the place. It consisted of an aged

cook who, as she bent over her cauldrons, looked like something out of a travelling company of " Macbeth," touring the smaller towns of the North, and Murgatroyd, the butler, a huge, sinister man with a cast in one eye and an evil light in the other.

Many men, under these conditions, would have been daunted. But not Wilfred Mulliner. Apart from the fact that, like all the Mulliners, he was as brave as a lion, he had come expecting something of this nature. He settled down to his duties and kept his eyes open, and before long his vigilance was rewarded.

One day, as he lurked about the dim-lit passage-ways, he saw Sir Jasper coming up the stairs with a laden tray in his hands. It contained a toast-rack, a half bot. of white wine, pepper, salt, veg., and in a covered dish something which Wilfred, sniffing cautiously, decided was a cutlet.

Lurking in the shadows, he followed the baronet to the top of the house. Sir Jasper paused at a door on the second floor. He knocked. The door opened, a hand was stretched forth, the tray vanished, the door closed, and the baronet moved away.

So did Wilfred. He had seen what he had wanted to see, discovered what he had wanted to discover. He returned to the servants' hall, and under the gloomy eyes of Murgatroyd began to shape his plans.

" Where you been ? " demanded the butler, suspiciously.

" Oh, hither and thither," said Wilfred, with a well-assumed airiness.

Murgatroyd directed a menacing glance at him.

" You'd better stay where you belong," he said, in his thick, growling voice. " There's things in this house that don't want seeing."

" Ah ! " agreed the cook, dropping an onion in the cauldron.

Wilfred could not repress a shudder.

But, even as he shuddered, he was conscious of a certain relief. At least, he reflected, they were not starving his darling. That cutlet had smelt uncommonly good : and, if the bill of fare was always maintained at this level, she had nothing to complain of in the catering.

But his relief was short-lived. What, after all, he asked himself, are cutlets to a girl who is imprisoned in a locked room of a sinister country-house and is being forced to marry a man she does not love ? Practically nothing. When the heart is sick, cutlets merely alleviate, they do not cure. Fiercely Wilfred told himself that, come what might, few days should pass before he found the key to that locked door and bore away his love to freedom and happiness.

The only obstacle in the way of this scheme was that it was plainly going to be a matter of the greatest difficulty to find the key. That night, when his employer dined, Wilfred searched his room thoroughly. He found nothing. The key, he was forced to conclude, was kept on the baronet's person.

Then how to secure it ?

It is not too much to say that Wilfred Mulliner was non-plussed. The brain which had electrified the world of Science by discovering that if you mixed a stiffish oxygen and potassium and added a splash of tri-nitrotoluol and a spot of old brandy you got something that could be sold in America as champagne at a hundred and fifty dollars the case, had to confess itself baffled.

To attempt to analyse the young man's

emotions, as the next week dragged itself by, would be merely morbid. Life cannot, of course, be all sunshine : and in relating a story like this, which is a slice of life, one must pay as much attention to shade as to light : nevertheless, it would be tedious were I to describe to you in detail the soul-torments which afflicted Wilfred Mulliner as day followed day and no solution to the problem presented itself. You are all intelligent men, and you can picture to yourselves how a high-spirited young fellow, deeply in love, must have felt ; knowing that the girl he loved was languishing in what practically amounted to a dungeon, though situated on an upper floor, and chafing at his inability to set her free.

His eyes became sunken. His cheek-bones stood out. He lost weight. And so noticeable was this change in his physique that Sir Jasper ffinch-ffarrowmere commented on it one evening in tones of unconcealed envy.

"How the devil, Straker," he said—for this was the pseudonym under which Wilfred was passing, " do you manage to keep so thin ? Judging by the weekly books, you eat like a starving Esquimaux, and yet you don't put

on weight. Now I, in addition to knocking
off butter and potatoes, have started drink-
ing hot unsweetened lemon-juice each night
before retiring : and yet, damme," he said
—for, like all baronets, he was careless in
his language, " I weighed myself this morning, and I was up another six ounces. What's
the explanation ? "

" Yes, Sir Jasper," said Wilfred, mechani-
cally.

" What the devil do you mean, Yes, Sir
Jasper ? "

" No, Sir Jasper."

The baronet wheezed plaintively.

" I've been studying this matter closely,"
he said, " and it's one of the seven wonders
of the world. Have you ever seen a fat
valet ? Of course not. Nor has anybody
else. There is no such thing as a fat valet.
And yet there is scarcely a moment during
the day when a valet is not eating. He
rises at six-thirty, and at seven is having
coffee and buttered toast. At eight, he
breakfasts off porridge, cream, eggs, bacon,
jam, bread, butter, more eggs, more bacon,
more jam, more tea, and more butter,
finishing up with a slice of cold ham and a

sardine. At eleven o'clock he has his
'elevenses,' consisting of coffee, cream, more
bread and more butter. At one, luncheon
—a hearty meal, replete with every form of
starchy food and lots of beer. If he can get
at the port, he has port. At three, a snack.
At four, another snack. At five, tea and
buttered toast. At seven—dinner, probably
with floury potatoes, and certainly with lots
more beer. At nine, another snack. And
at ten-thirty he retires to bed, taking with
him a glass of milk and a plate of biscuits to
keep himself from getting hungry in the night.
And yet he remains as slender as a string-
bean, while I, who have been dieting for
years, tip the beam at two hundred and
seventeen pounds, and am growing a third
and supplementary chin. These are mys-
teries, Straker.''

" Yes, Sir Jasper.''

" Well, I'll tell you one thing,'' said the
baronet, " I'm getting down one of those
indoor Turkish Bath cabinet-affairs from
London ; and if that doesn't do the trick, I
give up the struggle.''

The indoor Turkish Bath duly arrived and

was unpacked ; and it was some three nights later that Wilfred, brooding in the servants' hall, was aroused from his reverie by Murgatroyd.

"Here," said Murgatroyd, "wake up. Sir Jasper's calling you."

"Calling me what ? " asked Wilfred, coming to himself with a start.

"Calling you very loud," growled the butler.

It was indeed so. From the upper regions of the house there was proceeding a series of sharp yelps, evidently those of a man in mortal stress. Wilfred was reluctant to interfere in any way if, as seemed probable, his employer was dying in agony ; but he was a conscientious man, and it was his duty, while in this sinister house, to perform the work for which he was paid. He hurried up the stairs ; and, entering Sir Jasper's bedroom, perceived the baronet's crimson face protruding from the top of the indoor Turkish Bath.

"So you've come at last ! " cried Sir Jasper. "Look here, when you put me into this infernal contrivance just now, what did you do to the dashed thing ? "

" Nothing beyond what was indicated in the printed pamphlet accompanying the machine, Sir Jasper. Following the instructions, I slid Rod A into Groove B, fastening with Catch C—— "

" Well, you must have made a mess of it, somehow. The thing's stuck. I can't get out."

" You can't ? " cried Wilfred.

" No.   And the bally apparatus is getting considerably hotter than the hinges of the Inferno."   I must apologise for Sir Jasper's language, but you know what baronets are. " I'm being cooked to a crisp."

A sudden flash of light seemed to blaze upon Wilfred Mulliner.

" I will release you, Sir Jasper—— "

" Well, hurry up, then."

" On one condition."   Wilfred fixed him with a piercing gaze.   " First, I must have the key."

" There isn't a key, you idiot.   It doesn't lock.   It just clicks when you slide Gadget D into Thingummybob E."

" The key I require is that of the room in which you are holding Angela Purdue a prisoner."

" What the devil do you mean ? Ouch ! "

" I will tell you what I mean, Sir Jasper ffinch-ffarrowmere. I am Wilfred Mulliner ! "

" Don't be an ass. Wilfred Mulliner has black hair. Yours is red. You must be thinking of some one else."

" This is a wig," said Wilfred. " By Clarkson." He shook a menacing finger at the baronet. " You little thought, Sir Jasper ffinch-ffarrowmere, when you embarked on this dastardly scheme, that Wilfred Mulliner was watching your every move. I guessed your plans from the start. And now is the moment when I checkmate them. Give me that key, you Fiend."

" ffiend," corrected Sir Jasper, automatically.

" I am going to release my darling, to take her away from this dreadful house, to marry her by special licence as soon as it can legally be done."

In spite of his sufferings, a ghastly laugh escaped Sir Jasper's lips.

" You are, are you ! "

" I am."

" Yes, you are ! "

" Give me the key."

" I haven't got it, you chump. It's in the door."

" Ha, ha ! "

" It's no good saying ' Ha, ha ! ' It is in the door. On Angela's side of the door."

" A likely story ! But I cannot stay here wasting time. If you will not give me the key, I shall go up and break in the door."

" Do ! " Once more the baronet laughed like a tortured soul. " And see what she'll say."

Wilfred could make nothing of this last remark. He could, he thought, imagine very clearly what Angela would say. He could picture her sobbing on his chest, murmuring that she knew he would come, that she had never doubted him for an instant. He leapt for the door.

" Here ! Hi ! Aren't you going to let me out ? "

" Presently," said Wilfred. " Keep cool." He raced up the stairs.

" Angela," he cried, pressing his lips against the panel. " Angela ! "

" Who's that ? " answered a well-remembered voice from within.

"It is I—Wilfred. I am going to burst open the door. Stand clear of the gates."

He drew back a few paces, and hurled himself at the woodwork. There was a grinding crash, as the lock gave. And Wilfred, staggering on, found himself in a room so dark that he could see nothing.

"Angela, where are you?"

"I'm here. And I'd like to know why you are, after that letter I wrote you. Some men," continued the strangely cold voice, "do not seem to know how to take a hint."

Wilfred staggered, and would have fallen had he not clutched at his forehead.

"That letter?" he stammered. "You surely didn't mean what you wrote in that letter?"

"I meant every word and I wish I had put in more."

"But—but—but—— But don't you love me, Angela?"

A hard, mocking laugh rang through the room.

"Love you? Love the man who recommended me to try Mulliner's Raven Gipsy Face-Cream!"

"What do you mean?"

" I will tell you what I mean. Wilfred
Mulliner, look on your handiwork ! "

The room became suddenly flooded with
light. And there, standing with her hand
on the switch, stood Angela—a queenly,
lovely figure, in whose radiant beauty the
sternest critic would have noted but one
flaw—the fact that she was piebald.

Wilfred gazed at her with adoring eyes.
Her face was partly brown and partly white,
and on her snowy neck were patches of sepia
that looked like the thumb-prints you find
on the pages of books in the Free Library :
but he thought her the most beautiful
creature he had ever seen. He longed to
fold her in his arms : and but for the fact
that her eyes told him that she would
undoubtedly land an upper-cut on him if
he tried it he would have done so.

" Yes," she went on, " this is what you
have made of me, Wilfred Mulliner—you and
that awful stuff you call the Raven Gipsy
Face-Cream. This is the skin you loved to
touch ! I took your advice and bought one
of the large jars at seven and six, and see
the result ! Barely twenty-four hours after
the first application, I could have walked

into any circus and named my own terms as the Spotted Princess of the Fiji Islands. I fled here to my childhood home, to hide myself. And the first thing that happened" —her voice broke—" was that my favourite hunter shied at me and tried to bite pieces out of his manger : while Ponto, my little dog, whom I have reared from a puppy, caught one sight of my face and is now in the hands of the vet. and unlikely to recover. And it was you, Wilfred Mulliner, who brought this curse upon me ! "

Many men would have wilted beneath these searing words, but Wilfred Mulliner merely smiled with infinite compassion and understanding.

" It is quite all right," he said. " I should have warned you, sweetheart, that this occasionally happens in cases where the skin is exceptionally delicate and finely-textured. It can be speedily remedied by an application of the Mulliner Snow of the Mountains Lotion, four shillings the medium-sized bottle."

" Wilfred ! Is this true ? "

" Perfectly true, dearest. And is this all that stands between us ? "

" No ! " shouted a voice of thunder.

Wilfred wheeled sharply. In the door-
way stood Sir Jasper ffinch-ffarrowmere.
He was swathed in a bath-towel, what was
visible of his person being a bright crimson.
Behind him, toying with a horse-whip, stood
Murgatroyd, the butler.

" You didn't expect to see me, did you ? "

" I certainly," replied Wilfred, severely,
" did not expect to see you in a lady's
presence in a costume like that."

" Never mind my costume." Sir Jasper
turned.

" Murgatroyd, do your duty ! "

The butler, scowling horribly, advanced
into the room.

" Stop ! " screamed Angela.

" I haven't begun yet, miss," said the
butler, deferentially.

" You shan't touch Wilfred. I love
him."

" What ! " cried Sir Jasper. " After all
that has happened ? "

" Yes. He has explained everything."

A grim frown appeared on the baronet's
vermilion face.

" I'll bet he hasn't explained why he left

me to be cooked in that infernal Turkish Bath. I was beginning to throw out clouds of smoke when Murgatroyd, faithful fellow, heard my cries and came and released me."

"Though not my work," added the butler.

Wilfred eyed him steadily.

"If," he said, "you used Mulliner's Reduc-o, the recognised specific for obesity, whether in the tabloid form at three shillings the tin, or as a liquid at five and six the flask, you would have no need to stew in Turkish Baths. Mulliner's Reduc-o, which contains no injurious chemicals, but is compounded purely of health-giving herbs, is guaranteed to remove excess weight, steadily and without weakening after-effects, at the rate of two pounds a week. As used by the nobility."

The glare of hatred faded from the baronet's eyes.

"Is that a fact ? " he whispered.

"It is."

"You guarantee it ? "

"All the Mulliner preparations are fully guaranteed."

"My boy ! " cried the baronet. He shook Wilfred by the hand. "Take her," he said, brokenly. "And with her my b-blessing."

A discreet cough sounded in the background.

"You haven't anything, by any chance, sir," asked Murgatroyd, "that's good for lumbago?"

"Mulliner's Ease-o will cure the most stubborn case in six days."

"Bless you, sir, bless you," sobbed Murgatroyd. "Where can I get it?"

"At all chemists."

"It catches me in the small of the back principally, sir."

"It need catch you no longer," said Wilfred.

There is little to add. Murgatroyd is now the most lissom butler in Yorkshire. Sir Jasper's weight is down under the fifteen stone and he is thinking of taking up hunting again. Wilfred and Angela are man and wife; and never, I am informed, have the wedding-bells of the old church at ffinch village rung out a blither peal than they did on that June morning when Angela, raising to her love a face on which the brown was as evenly distributed as on an antique walnut table, replied to the clergyman's question, "Wilt thou, Angela, take this

Wilfred ? " with a shy, " I will." They now have two bonny bairns—the small, or Percival, at a preparatory school in Sussex, and the large, or Ferdinand, at Eton.

Here Mr. Mulliner, having finished his hot Scotch, bade us farewell and took his departure.

A silence followed his exit. The company seemed plunged in deep thought. Then somebody rose.

" Well, good night all," he said.

It seemed to sum up the situation

III

MULLINER'S BUCK-U-UPPO

THE village Choral Society had been giving a performance of Gilbert and Sullivan's "Sorcerer" in aid of the Church Organ Fund ; and, as we sat in the window of the Anglers' Rest, smoking our pipes, the audience came streaming past us down the little street. Snatches of song floated to our ears, and Mr. Mulliner began to croon in unison.

" ' Ah me ! I was a pa-ale you-oung curate then ! ' " chanted Mr. Mulliner in the rather snuffling voice in which the amateur singer seems to find it necessary to render the old songs.

" Remarkable," he said, resuming his natural tones, " how fashions change, even in clergymen. There are very few pale young curates nowadays."

" True," I agreed. " Most of them are

beefy young fellows who rowed for their colleges. I don't believe I have ever seen a pale young curate."

" You never met my nephew Augustine, I think ? "

" Never."

" The description in the song would have fitted him perfectly. You will want to hear all about my nephew Augustine."

At the time of which I am speaking (said Mr. Mulliner) my nephew Augustine was a curate, and very young and extremely pale. As a boy he had completely outgrown his strength, and I rather think that at his Theological College some of the wilder spirits must have bullied him ; for when he went to Lower Briskett-in-the-Midden to assist the vicar, the Rev. Stanley Brandon, in his cure of souls, he was as meek and mild a young man as you could meet in a day's journey. He had flaxen hair, weak blue eyes, and the general demeanour of a saintly but timid codfish. Precisely, in short, the sort of young curate who seems to have been so common in the 'eighties, or whenever it was that Gilbert wrote "The Sorcerer."

The personality of his immediate superior did little or nothing to help him to overcome his native diffidence. The Rev. Stanley Brandon was a huge and sinewy man of violent temper, whose red face and glittering eyes might well have intimidated the toughest curate. The Rev. Stanley had been a heavy-weight boxer at Cambridge, and I gather from Augustine that he seemed to be always on the point of introducing into debates on parish matters the methods which had made him so successful in the roped ring. I remember Augustine telling me that once, on the occasion when he had ventured to oppose the other's views in the matter of decorating the church for the Harvest Festival, he thought for a moment that the vicar was going to drop him with a right hook to the chin. It was some quite trivial point that had come up—a question as to whether the pumpkin would look better in the apse or the clerestory, if I recollect rightly—but for several seconds it seemed as if blood was about to be shed.

Such was the Rev. Stanley Brandon. And yet it was to the daughter of this for-midable man that Augustine Mulliner had

permitted himself to lose his heart. Truly,
Cupid makes heroes of us all.

Jane was a very nice girl, and just as
fond of Augustine as he was of her. But,
as each lacked the nerve to go to the girl's
father and put him abreast of the position
of affairs, they were forced to meet sur-
reptitiously. This jarred upon Augustine,
who, like all the Mulliners, loved the truth
and hated any form of deception. And one
evening, as they paced beside the laurels at
the bottom of the vicarage garden, he
rebelled.

"My dearest," said Augustine, "I can
no longer brook this secrecy. I shall go
into the house immediately and ask your
father for your hand."

Jane paled and clung to his arm. She
knew so well that it was not her hand but
her father's foot which he would receive if
he carried out this mad scheme.

"No, no, Augustine! You must not!"

"But, darling, it is the only straight-
forward course."

"But not to-night. I beg of you, not
to-night."

"Why not?"

"Because father is in a very bad temper. He has just had a letter from the bishop, rebuking him for wearing too many orphreys on his chasuble, and it has upset him terribly. You see, he and the bishop were at school together, and father can never forget it. He said at dinner that if old Boko Bickerton thought he was going to order him about he would jolly well show him."

"And the bishop comes here to-morrow for the Confirmation services!" gasped Augustine.

"Yes. And I'm so afraid they will quarrel. It's such a pity father hasn't some other bishop over him. He always remembers that he once hit this one in the eye for pouring ink on his collar, and this lowers his respect for his spiritual authority. So you won't go in and tell him to-night, will you?"

"I will not," Augustine assured her with a slight shiver.

"And you will be sure to put your feet in hot mustard and water when you get home? The dew has made the grass so wet."

"I will indeed, dearest."

" You are not strong, you know."

" No, I am not strong."

" You ought to take some really good tonic."

" Perhaps I ought. Good night, Jane."

" Good night, Augustine."

The lovers parted.   Jane slipped back into the vicarage, and Augustine made his way to his cosy rooms in the High Street. And the first thing he noticed on entering was a parcel on the table, and beside it a letter.

He opened it listlessly, his thoughts far away.

" *My dear Augustine.*"

He turned to the last page and glanced at the signature. The letter was from his Aunt Angela, the wife of my brother, Wilfred Mulliner. You may remember that I once told you the story of how these two came together. If so, you will recall that my brother Wilfred was the eminent chemical researcher who had invented, among other specifics, such world-famous preparations as Mulliner's Raven Gipsy Face-Cream and the Mulliner Snow of the Mountains Lotion. He and Augustine had never been particularly intimate, but between Augustine and his

aunt there had always existed a warm
friendship.

My dear Augustine (wrote Angela Mulliner),
        *I have been thinking so much about
you lately, and I cannot forget that, when I
saw you last, you seemed very fragile and
deficient in vitamines.   I do hope you take
care of yourself.*

   *I have been feeling for some time that you
ought to take a tonic, and by a lucky chance
Wilfred has just invented one which he tells
me is the finest thing he has ever done.   It is
called Buck-U-Uppo, and acts directly on the
red corpuscles.   It is not yet on the market,
but I have managed to smuggle a sample
bottle from Wilfred's laboratory, and I want
you to try it at once.   I am sure it is just what
you need.*

                    *Your affectionate aunt,
                            Angela Mulliner.*

   *P.S.—You take a tablespoonful before going
to bed, and another just before breakfast.*

Augustine was not an unduly superstitious
young man, but the coincidence of this tonic

arriving so soon after Jane had told him that a tonic was what he needed affected him deeply. It seemed to him that this thing must have been meant. He shook the bottle, uncorked it, and, pouring out a liberal table-spoonful, shut his eyes and swallowed it.

The medicine, he was glad to find, was not unpleasant to the taste. It had a slightly pungent flavour, rather like old boot-soles beaten up in sherry. Having taken the dose, he read for a while in a book of theo-logical essays, and then went to bed.

And as his feet slipped between the sheets, he was annoyed to find that Mrs. Wardle, his housekeeper, had once more forgotten his hot-water bottle.

" Oh, dash ! " said Augustine.

He was thoroughly upset. He had told the woman over and over again that he suffered from cold feet and could not get to sleep unless the dogs were properly warmed up. He sprang out of bed and went to the head of the stairs.

" Mrs. Wardle ! " he cried.

There was no reply.

" Mrs. Wardle ! " bellowed Augustine in a voice that rattled the window-panes like a strong nor'-easter. Until to-night he had always been very much afraid of his housekeeper and had both walked and talked softly in her presence. But now he was conscious of a strange new fortitude. His head was singing a little, and he felt equal to a dozen Mrs. Wardles.

Shuffling footsteps made themselves heard.

" Well, what is it now ? " asked a querulous voice.

Augustine snorted.

" I'll tell you what it is now," he roared. " How many times have I told you always to put a hot-water bottle in my bed ? You've forgotten it again, you old clothhead ! "

Mrs. Wardle peered up, astounded and militant.

" Mr. Mulliner, I am not accustomed—— "

" Shut up ! " thundered Augustine. " What I want from you is less back-chat and more hot-water bottles. Bring it up at once, or I leave to-morrow. Let me endeavour to get it into your concrete skull that you aren't the only person letting rooms in this village. Any more lip and I walk straight round the corner, where I'll be appreciated. Hot-water bottle ho! And look slippy about it."

"Yes, Mr. Mulliner. Certainly, Mr. Mulliner. In one moment, Mr. Mulliner."

"Action! Action!" boomed Augustine. "Show some speed. Put a little snap into it."

"Yes, yes, most decidedly, Mr. Mulliner," replied the chastened voice from below.

An hour later, as he was dropping off to sleep, a thought crept into Augustine's mind. Had he not been a little brusque with Mrs. Wardle? Had there not been in his manner something a shade abrupt—almost rude? Yes, he decided regretfully, there had. He lit a candle and reached for the diary which lay on the table at his bedside.

He made an entry.

The meek shall inherit the earth. Am I sufficiently meek? I wonder. This evening, when reproaching Mrs. Wardle, my worthy housekeeper, for omitting to place a hot-water bottle in my bed, I spoke quite crossly. The provocation was severe, but still I was surely to blame for allowing my passions to run riot. Mem: Must guard agst this.

But when he woke next morning, different feelings prevailed. He took his ante-breakfast dose of Buck-U-Uppo : and looking at the entry in the diary, could scarcely believe that it was he who had written it. " Quite cross ? " Of course he had been quite cross. Wouldn't anybody be quite cross who was for ever being persecuted by beetle-wits who forgot hot-water bottles ?

Erasing the words with one strong dash of a thick-leaded pencil, he scribbled in the margin a hasty " Mashed potatoes ! Served the old idiot right ! " and went down to breakfast.

He felt most amazingly fit. Undoubtedly, in asserting that this tonic of his acted forcefully upon the red corpuscles, his Uncle Wilfred had been right. Until that moment Augustine had never supposed that he had any red corpuscles ; but now, as he sat waiting for Mrs. Wardle to bring him his fried egg, he could feel them dancing about all over him. They seemed to be forming rowdy parties and sliding down his spine. His eyes sparkled, and from sheer joy of living he sang a few bars from the hymn for those of riper years at sea.

He was still singing when Mrs. Wardle entered with a dish.

" What's this ? " demanded Augustine, eyeing it dangerously.

" A nice fried egg, sir."

" And what, pray, do you mean by nice ? It may be an amiable egg. It may be a civil, well-meaning egg. But if you think it is fit for human consumption, adjust that impression. Go back to your kitchen, woman ; select another ; and remember this time that you are a cook, not an incinerating machine. Between an egg that is fried and an egg that is cremated there is a wide and substantial difference. This difference, if you wish to retain me as a lodger in these far too expensive rooms, you will endeavour to appreciate."

The glowing sense of well-being with which Augustine had begun the day did not diminish with the passage of time. It seemed, indeed, to increase. So full of effervescing energy did the young man feel that, departing from his usual custom of spending the morning crouched over the fire, he picked up his hat, stuck it at a rakish angle on his head, and sallied out for a healthy tramp across the fields.

It was while he was returning, flushed and rosy, that he observed a sight which is rare in the country districts of England— the spectacle of a bishop running. It is not often in a place like Lower Briskett-in-the-Midden that you see a bishop at all; and when you do he is either riding in a stately car or pacing at a dignified walk. This one was sprinting like a Derby winner, and Augustine paused to drink in the sight.

The bishop was a large, burly bishop, built for endurance rather than speed; but he was making excellent going. He flashed past Augustine in a whirl of flying gaiters: and then, proving himself thereby no mere specialist but a versatile all-round athlete, suddenly dived for a tree and climbed rapidly into its branches. His motive, Augustine readily divined, was to elude a rough, hairy dog which was toiling in his wake. The dog reached the tree a moment after his quarry had climbed it, and stood there, barking.

Augustine strolled up.

" Having a little trouble with the dumb friend, bish ? " he asked, genially.

The bishop peered down from his eyrie.

" Young man," he said, " save me ! "

" Right most indubitably ho ! " replied Augustine. " Leave it to me."

Until to-day he had always been terrified of dogs, but now he did not hesitate. Almost quicker than words can tell, he picked up a stone, discharged it at the animal, and whooped cheerily as it got home with a thud. The dog, knowing when he had had enough, removed himself at some forty-five m.p.h. ; and the bishop, descending cautiously, clasped Augustine's hand in his.

" My preserver ! " said the bishop.

" Don't give it another thought," said Augustine, cheerily. " Always glad to do a pal a good turn. We clergymen must stick together."

" I thought he had me for a minute."

" Quite a nasty customer. Full of rude energy."

The bishop nodded.

" His eye was not dim, nor his natural force abated. Deuteronomy xxxiv. 7," he agreed. " I wonder if you can direct me to the vicarage ? I fear I have come a little out of my way."

" I'll take you there."

" Thank you. Perhaps it would be as

well if you did not come in. I have a serious matter to discuss with old Pieface—I mean, with the Rev. Stanley Brandon."

" I have a serious matter to discuss with his daughter. I'll just hang about the garden."

" You are a very excellent young man," said the bishop, as they walked along. " You are a curate, eh ? "

" At present. But," said Augustine, tapping his companion on the chest, " just watch my smoke. That's all I ask you to do—just watch my smoke."

" I will. You should rise to great heights —to the very top of the tree."

" Like you did just now, eh ? Ha, ha ! "

" Ha, ha ! " said the bishop. " You young rogue ! "

He poked Augustine in the ribs.

" Ha, ha, ha ! " said Augustine.

He slapped the bishop on the back.

" But all joking aside," said the bishop as they entered the vicarage grounds, " I really shall keep my eye on you and see that you receive the swift preferment which your talents and character deserve. I say to you, my dear young friend, speaking seriously and

weighing my words, that the way you picked
that dog off with that stone was the smoothest
thing I ever saw. And I am a man who
always tells the strict truth."

" Great is truth and mighty above all
things. Esdras iv. 41," said Augustine.

He turned away and strolled towards the
laurel bushes, which were his customary
meeting-place with Jane. The bishop went
on to the front door and rang the bell.

Although they had made no definite
appointment, Augustine was surprised when
the minutes passed and no Jane appeared.
He did not know that she had been told off
by her father to entertain the bishop's wife
that morning, and show her the sights of
Lower Briskett-in-the-Midden. He waited
some quarter of an hour with growing
impatience, and was about to leave when
suddenly from the house there came to his
ears the sound of voices raised angrily.

He stopped. The voices appeared to
proceed from a room on the ground floor
facing the garden.

Running lightly over the turf, Augustine
paused outside the window and listened.

The window was open at the bottom, and he could hear quite distinctly.

The vicar was speaking in a voice that vibrated through the room.

" Is that so ? " said the vicar.

" Yes, it is ! " said the bishop.

" Ha, ha ! "

" Ha, ha ! to you, and see how you like it ! " rejoined the bishop with spirit.

Augustine drew a step closer. It was plain that Jane's fears had been justified and that there was serious trouble afoot between these two old schoolfellows. He peeped in. The vicar, his hands behind his coat-tails, was striding up and down the carpet, while the bishop, his back to the fireplace, glared defiance at him from the hearth-rug.

" Who ever told you you were an authority on chasubles ? " demanded the vicar.

" That's all right who told me," rejoined the bishop.

" I don't believe you know what a chasuble is."

" Is that so ? "

" Well, what is it, then ? "

" It's a circular cloak hanging from the shoulders, elaborately embroidered with a pattern and with orphreys. And you can argue as much as you like, young Pieface, but you can't get away from the fact that there are too many orphreys on yours. And what I'm telling you is that you've jolly well got to switch off a few of those orphreys or you'll get it in the neck."

The vicar's eyes glittered furiously.

" Is that so ? " he said. " Well, I just won't, so there ! And it's like your cheek coming here and trying to high-hat me. You seem to have forgotten that I knew you when you were an inky-faced kid at school, and that, if I liked, I could tell the world one or two things about you which would probably amuse it."

" My past is an open book."

" Is it ? " The vicar laughed male-volently. " Who put the white mouse in the French master's desk ? "

The bishop started.

" Who put jam in the dormitory prefect's bed ? " he retorted.

" Who couldn't keep his collar clean ? "

" Who used to wear a dickey ? " The bishop's wonderful organ-like voice, whose softest whisper could be heard throughout a

vast cathedral, rang out in tones of thunder.
" Who was sick at the house supper ? "

The vicar quivered from head to foot.
His rubicund face turned a deeper crimson.

" You know jolly well," he said, in
shaking accents, " that there was something
wrong with the turkey. Might have upset
any one."

" The only thing wrong with the turkey
was that you ate too much of it. If you
had paid as much attention to developing
your soul as you did to developing your
tummy, you might by now," said the bishop,
" have risen to my own eminence."

" Oh, might I ? "

" No, perhaps I am wrong. You never
had the brain."

The vicar uttered another discordant laugh.

" Brain is good ! We know all about your
eminence, as you call it, and how you rose
to that eminence."

" What do you mean ? "

" You are a bishop. How you became
one we will not inquire."

" What do you mean ? "

" What I say. We will not inquire."

" Why don't you inquire ? "

" Because," said the vicar, " it is better
not ! "

The bishop's self-control left him.   His
face contorted with fury, he took a step
forward.   And   simultaneously   Augustine
sprang lightly into the room.

" Now, now, now ! " said Augustine.
" Now, now, now, now, now ! "

The two men stood transfixed.   They
stared at the intruder dumbly.

" Come, come ! " said Augustine.

The vicar was the first to recover.   He
glowered at Augustine.

" What do you mean by jumping through
my window ? " he thundered.   " Are you a
curate or a harlequin ? "

Augustine met his gaze with an unfaltering
eye.

" I am a curate," he replied, with a
dignity that well became him.   " And, as a
curate, I cannot stand by and see two
superiors of the cloth, who are moreover
old schoolfellows, forgetting themselves.   It
isn't right.   Absolutely not right, my dear
old superiors of the cloth."

The vicar bit his lip.   The bishop bowed
his head.

" Listen," proceeded Augustine, placing a hand on the shoulder of each. " I hate to see you two dear good chaps quarrelling like this."

" He started it," said the vicar, sullenly.

" Never mind who started it." Augustine silenced the bishop with a curt gesture as he made to speak. " Be sensible, my dear fellows. Respect the decencies of debate. Exercise a little good-humoured give-and-take. You say," he went on, turning to the bishop, " that our good friend here has too many orphreys on his chasuble ? "

" I do. And I stick to it."

" Yes, yes, yes. But what," said Augustine, soothingly, " are a few orphreys between friends ? Reflect ! You and our worthy vicar here were at school together. You are bound by the sacred ties of the old Alma Mater. With him you sported on the green. With him you shared a crib and threw inked darts in the hour supposed to be devoted to the study of French. Do these things mean nothing to you ? Do these memories touch no chord ? " He turned appealingly from one to the other. " Vicar ! Bish ! "

The vicar had moved away and was wiping his eyes. The bishop fumbled for a pocket-handkerchief. There was a silence.

"Sorry, Pieface," said the bishop, in a choking voice.

"Shouldn't have spoken as I did, Boko," mumbled the vicar.

"If you want to know what I think," said the bishop, "you are right in attributing your indisposition at the house supper to something wrong with the turkey. I recollect saying at the time that the bird should never have been served in such a condition."

"And when you put that white mouse in the French master's desk," said the vicar, "you performed one of the noblest services to humanity of which there is any record. They ought to have made you a bishop on the spot."

"Pieface!"

"Boko!"

The two men clasped hands.

"Splendid!" said Augustine. "Everything hotsy-totsy now?"

"Quite, quite," said the vicar.

"As far as I am concerned, completely

hotsy-totsy," said the bishop. He turned to his old friend solicitously. " You will continue to wear all the orphreys you want— will you not, Pieface ? "

" No, no. I see now that I was wrong. From now on, Boko, I abandon orphreys altogether."

" But, Pieface—— "

" It's all right," the vicar assured him. " I can take them or leave them alone."

" Splendid fellow ! " The bishop coughed to hide his emotion, and there was another silence. " I think, perhaps," he went on, after a pause, " I should be leaving you now, my dear chap, and going in search of my wife. She is with your daughter, I believe, somewhere in the village."

" They are coming up the drive now."

" Ah, yes, I see them. A charming girl, your daughter."

Augustine clapped him on the shoulder.

" Bish," he exclaimed, " you said a mouthful. She is the dearest, sweetest girl in the whole world. And I should be glad, vicar, if you would give your consent to our immediate union. I love Jane with a good man's fervour, and I am happy to inform you that my sentiments are returned. Assure us, therefore, of your approval, and I will go at once and have the banns put up."

The vicar leaped as though he had been stung. Like so many vicars, he had a poor opinion of curates, and he had always regarded Augustine as rather below than above the general norm or level of the despised class.

" What ! " he cried.

" A most excellent idea," said the bishop, beaming. " A very happy notion, I call it."

" My daughter ! " The vicar seemed dazed. " My daughter marry a curate ! "

" You were a curate once yourself, Pie-face."

" Yes, but not a curate like that."

" No ! " said the bishop. " You were not. Nor was I. Better for us both had we been. This young man, I would have you know, is the most outstandingly ex-cellent young man I have ever encountered. Are you aware that scarcely an hour ago he saved me with the most consummate address from a large shaggy dog with black spots and

a kink in his tail ? I was sorely pressed,
Pieface, when this young man came up and,
with a readiness of resource and an accuracy
of aim which it would be impossible to over-
praise, got that dog in the short ribs with a
rock and sent him flying."

The vicar seemed to be struggling with
some powerful emotion. His eyes had
widened.

" A dog with black spots ? "

" Very black spots. But no blacker, I
fear, than the heart they hid."

" And he really plugged him in the short
ribs ? "

" As far as I could see, squarely in the
short ribs."

The vicar held out his hand.

" Mulliner," he said, " I was not aware
of this. In the light of the facts which have
just been drawn to my attention, I have no
hesitation in saying that my objections are
removed. I have had it in for that dog
since the second Sunday before Septuagesima,
when he pinned me by the ankle as I paced
beside the river composing a sermon on
Certain Alarming Manifestations of the So-
called Modern Spirit. Take Jane. I give

my consent freely. And may she be as happy as any girl with such a husband ought to be."

A few more affecting words were exchanged, and then the bishop and Augustine left the house. The bishop was silent and thoughtful.

" I owe you a great deal, Mulliner," he said at length.

" Oh, I don't know," said Augustine. " Would you say that ? "

" A very great deal. You saved me from a terrible disaster. Had you not leaped through that window at that precise juncture and intervened, I really believe I should have pasted my dear old friend Brandon in the eye. I was sorely exasperated."

" Our good vicar can be trying at times," agreed Augustine.

" My fist was already clenched, and I was just hauling off for the swing when you checked me. What the result would have been, had you not exhibited a tact and discretion beyond your years, I do not like to think. I might have been unfrocked." He shivered at the thought, though the weather was mild. " I could never have shown my face at the Athenæum again. But, tut, tut ! " went on the bishop, patting Augustine on the shoulder, " let us not dwell on what might have been. Speak to me of yourself. The vicar's charming daughter—you really love her ? "

" I do, indeed."

The bishop's face had grown grave.

" Think well, Mulliner," he said. " Marriage is a serious affair. Do not plunge into it without due reflection. I myself am a husband, and, though singularly blessed in the possession of a devoted helpmeet, cannot but feel sometimes that a man is better off as a bachelor. Women, Mulliner, are odd."

" True," said Augustine.

" My own dear wife is the best of women. And, as I never weary of saying, a good woman is a wondrous creature, cleaving to the right and the good under all change ; lovely in youthful comeliness, lovely all her life in comeliness of heart. And yet—— "

" And yet ? " said Augustine.

The bishop mused for a moment. He

wriggled a little with an expression of pain, and scratched himself between the shoulder-blades.

"Well, I'll tell you," said the bishop. " It is a warm and pleasant day to-day, is it not ? "

"Exceptionally clement," said Augustine.

"A fair, sunny day, made gracious by a temperate westerly breeze. And yet, Mulliner, if you will credit my statement, my wife insisted on my putting on my thick winter woollies this morning. Truly," sighed the bishop, " as a jewel of gold in a swine's snout, so is a fair woman which is without discretion. Proverbs xi. 21."

" Twenty-two," corrected Augustine.

" I should have said twenty-two. They are made of thick flannel, and I have an exceptionally sensitive skin. Oblige me, my dear fellow, by rubbing me in the small of the back with the ferrule of your stick. I think it will ease the irritation."

"But, my poor dear old bish," said Augustine, sympathetically, " this must not be.

The bishop shook his head ruefully.

"You would not speak so hardily,

D

Mulliner, if you knew my wife. There is no appeal from her decrees."

"Nonsense," cried Augustine, cheerily. He looked through the trees to where the lady bishopess, escorted by Jane, was examining a lobelia through her lorgnette with just the right blend of cordiality and condescension. "I'll fix that for you in a second."

The bishop clutched at his arm.

"My boy! What are you going to do?"

"I'm just going to have a word with your wife and put the matter up to her as a reasonable woman. Thick winter woollies on a day like this! Absurd!" said Augustine. "Preposterous! I never heard such rot."

The bishop gazed after him with a laden heart. Already he had come to love this young man like a son: and to see him charging so light-heartedly into the very jaws of destruction afflicted him with a deep and poignant sadness. He knew what his wife was like when even the highest in the land attempted to thwart her; and this brave lad was but a curate. In another moment

she would be looking at him through her
lorgnette : and England was littered with
the shrivelled remains of curates at whom
the lady bishopess had looked through her
lorgnette. He had seen them wilt like salted
slugs at the episcopal breakfast-table.

He held his breath. Augustine had
reached the lady bishopess, and the lady
bishopess was even now raising her lorgnette.

The bishop shut his eyes and turned
away. And then—years afterwards, it
seemed to him—a cheery voice hailed him :
and, turning, he perceived Augustine bounding back through the trees.

" It's all right, bish," said Augustine.

" All—all right ? " faltered the bishop.

" Yes. She says you can go and change
into the thin cashmere."

The bishop reeled.

" But—but—but what did you say to
her ? What arguments did you employ ? "

" Oh, I just pointed out what a warm day
it was and jollied her along a bit—— "

" Jollied her along a bit ! "

" And she agreed in the most friendly and
cordial manner. She has asked me to call
at the Palace one of these days."

The bishop seized Augustine's hand.

"My boy," he said in a broken voice, "you shall do more than call at the Palace. You shall come and live at the Palace. Become my secretary, Mulliner, and name your own salary. If you intend to marry, you will require an increased stipend. Become my secretary, boy, and never leave my side. I have needed somebody like you for years."

It was late in the afternoon when Augustine returned to his rooms, for he had been invited to lunch at the vicarage and had been the life and soul of the cheery little party.

"A letter for you, sir," said Mrs. Wardle, obsequiously.

Augustine took the letter.

"I am sorry to say I shall be leaving you shortly, Mrs. Wardle."

"Oh, sir! If there's anything I can do——"

"Oh, it's not that. The fact is, the bishop has made me his secretary, and I shall have to shift my toothbrush and spats to the Palace, you see."

" Well, fancy that, sir ! Why, you'll be a bishop yourself one of these days."

" Possibly," said Augustine. " Possibly. And now let me read this."

He opened the letter. A thoughtful frown appeared on his face as he read.

My dear Augustine,

I am writing in some haste to tell you that the impulsiveness of your aunt has led to a rather serious mistake.

She tells me that she dispatched to you yesterday by parcels post a sample bottle of my new Buck-U-Uppo, which she obtained without my knowledge from my laboratory. Had she mentioned what she was intending to do, I could have prevented a very unfortunate occurrence.

Mulliner's Buck-U-Uppo is of two grades or qualities—the A and the B. The A is a mild, but strengthening, tonic designed for human invalids. The B, on the other hand, is purely for circulation in the animal kingdom, and was invented to fill a long-felt want throughout our Indian possessions.

As you are doubtless aware, the favourite pastime of the Indian Maharajahs is the hunting of the tiger of the jungle from the backs of elephants ; and it has happened frequently in the past that hunts have been spoiled by the failure of the elephant to see eye to eye with its owner in the matter of what constitutes sport.

Too often elephants, on sighting the tiger, have turned and galloped home : and it was to correct this tendency on their part that I invented Mulliner's Buck-U-Uppo " B." One teaspoonful of the Buck-U-Uppo " B " administered in its morning bran-mash will cause the most timid elephant to trumpet loudly and charge the fiercest tiger without a qualm.

Abstain, therefore, from taking any of the contents of the bottle you now possess,

And believe me,

Your affectionate uncle,

Wilfred Mulliner.

Augustine remained for some time in deep thought after perusing this communication. Then, rising, he whistled a few bars of the psalm appointed for the twenty-sixth of June and left the room.

Half an hour later a telegraphic message was speeding over the wires.

It ran as follows :—

Wilfred Mulliner,
       The Gables,
              Lesser Lossingham,
                     Salop.

*Letter received.   Send immediately, C.O.D.,
three cases of the " B."   " Blessed shall be thy
basket and thy store."   Deuteronomy xxviii. 5.*
                              Augustine.

IV

THE BISHOP'S MOVE

ANOTHER Sunday was drawing to a close, and Mr. Mulliner had come into the bar - parlour of the Anglers' Rest wearing on his head, in place of the seedy old wideawake which usually adorned it, a glistening top hat. From this, combined with the sober black of his costume and the rather devout voice in which he ordered hot Scotch and lemon, I deduced that he had been attending Evensong.

" Good sermon ? " I asked.

" Quite good. The new curate preached. He seems a nice young fellow."

" Speaking of curates," I said, " I have often wondered what became of your nephew —the one you were telling me about the other day."

" Augustine ? "

" The fellow who took the Buck-U-Uppo."

" That was Augustine. And I am pleased and not a little touched," said Mr. Mulliner, beaming, " that you should have remembered the trivial anecdote which I related. In this self-centred world one does not always find such a sympathetic listener to one's stories. Let me see, where did we leave Augustine ? "

" He had just become the bishop's secretary and gone to live at the Palace."

"Ah, yes. We will take up his career, then, some six months after the date which you have indicated."

It was the custom of the good Bishop of Stortford—for, like all the prelates of our Church, he loved his labours—to embark upon the duties of the day (said Mr. Mulliner) in a cheerful and jocund spirit. Usually, as he entered his study to dispatch such business as might have arisen from the correspondence which had reached the Palace by the first post, there was a smile upon his face and possibly upon his lips a snatch of some gay psalm. But on the morning on which this story begins an observer would have noted that he wore a preoccupied, even

D 2

a sombre, look. Reaching the study door, he hesitated as if reluctant to enter ; then, pulling himself together with a visible effort, he turned the handle.

"Good morning, Mulliner, my boy," he said. His manner was noticeably embarrassed.

Augustine glanced brightly up from the pile of letters which he was opening.

"Cheerio, Bish. How's the lumbago to-day ? "

"I find the pain sensibly diminished, thank you, Mulliner—in fact, almost non-existent. This pleasant weather seems to do me good. For lo ! the winter is past, the rain is over and gone ; the flowers appear on the earth ; the time of the singing birds is come, and the voice of the turtle is heard in the land. Song of Solomon ii. 11, 12."

"Good work," said Augustine. "Well, there's nothing much of interest in these letters so far. The Vicar of St. Beowulf's in the West wants to know, How about incense ? "

"Tell him he mustn't."

"Right ho."

The bishop stroked his chin uneasily.

He seemed to be nerving himself for some unpleasant task.

"Mulliner," he said.

"Hullo?"

"Your mention of the word 'vicar' provides a cue, which I must not ignore, for alluding to a matter which you and I had under advisement yesterday — the matter of the vacant living of Steeple Mummery."

"Yes?" said Augustine eagerly. "Do I click?"

A spasm of pain passed across the bishop's face. He shook his head sadly.

"Mulliner, my boy," he said. "You know that I look upon you as a son and that, left to my own initiative, I would bestow this vacant living on you without a moment's hesitation. But an unforeseen complication has arisen. Unhappy lad, my wife has instructed me to give the post to a cousin of hers. A fellow," said the bishop bitterly, "who bleats like a sheep and doesn't know an alb from a reredos."

Augustine, as was only natural, was conscious of a momentary pang of disappointment. But he was a Mulliner and a sportsman.

" Don't give it another thought, Bish,"
he said cordially. " I quite understand. I
don't say I hadn't hopes, but no doubt there
will be another along in a minute."

" You know how it is," said the bishop,
looking cautiously round to see that the
door was closed. " It is better to dwell
in a corner of the housetop than with a
brawling woman in a wide house. Proverbs
xxi. 9."

" A continual dropping in a very rainy
day and a contentious woman are alike.
Proverbs xxvii. 15," agreed Augustine.

" Exactly. How well you understand me,
Mulliner."

" Meanwhile," said Augustine, holding up
a letter, " here's something that calls for
attention. It's from a bird of the name of
Trevor Entwhistle."

" Indeed ? An old schoolfellow of mine.
He is now Headmaster of Harchester, the
foundation at which we both received our
early education. What does he say ? "

" He wants to know if you will run down
for a few days and unveil a statue which
they have just put up to Lord Hemel of
Hempstead."

" Another old schoolfellow. We called him Fatty."

" There's a postscript over the page. He says he still has a dozen of the '87 port."

The bishop pursed his lips.

" These earthly considerations do not weigh with me so much as old Catsmeat— as the Reverend Trevor Entwhistle seems to suppose. However, one must not neglect the call of the dear old school. We will certainly go."

" We ? "

" I shall require your company. I think you will like Harchester, Mulliner. A noble pile, founded by the seventh Henry."

" I know it well. A young brother of mine is there."

" Indeed ? Dear me," mused the bishop, " it must be twenty years and more since I last visited Harchester. I shall enjoy seeing the old, familiar scenes once again. After all, Mulliner, to whatever eminence we may soar, howsoever great may be the prizes which life has bestowed upon us, we never wholly lose our sentiment for the dear old school. It is our Alma Mater, Mulliner, the gentle mother that has set our hesitating footsteps on the—— "

" Absolutely," said Augustine.

" And, as we grow older, we see that never can we recapture the old, careless gaiety of our school days. Life was not complex then, Mulliner. Life in that halcyon period was free from problems. We were not faced with the necessity of disappointing our friends."

" Now listen, Bish," said Augustine cheerily, " if you're still worrying about that living, forget it. Look at me. I'm quite chirpy, aren't I ? "

The bishop sighed.

" I wish I had your sunny resilience, Mulliner. How do you manage it ? "

" Oh, I keep smiling, and take the Buck-U-Uppo daily."

" The Buck-U-Uppo ? "

" It's a tonic my uncle Wilfred invented. Works like magic."

" I must ask you to let me try it one of these days. For somehow, Mulliner, I am finding life a little grey. What on earth," said the bishop, half to himself and speaking peevishly, " they wanted to put up a statue to old Fatty for, I can't imagine. A fellow who used to throw inked darts at people. However," he continued, abruptly abandoning this train of thought, " that is neither here nor there. If the Board of Governors of Harchester College has decided that Lord Hemel of Hempstead has by his services in the public weal earned a statue, it is not for us to cavil. Write to Mr. Entwhistle, Mulliner, and say that I shall be delighted."

Although, as he had told Augustine, fully twenty years had passed since his last visit to Harchester, the bishop found, somewhat to his surprise, that little or no alteration had taken place in the grounds, buildings and personnel of the school. It seemed to him almost precisely the same as it had been on the day, forty-three years before, when he had first come there as a new boy.

There was the tuck-shop where, a lissom stripling with bony elbows, he had shoved and pushed so often in order to get near the counter and snaffle a jam-sandwich in the eleven o'clock recess. There were the baths, the fives courts, the football fields, the library, the gymnasium, the gravel, the chestnut trees,

all just as they had been when the only thing
he knew about bishops was that they wore
bootlaces in their hats.

The sole change that he could see was
that on the triangle of turf in front of the
library there had been erected a granite
pedestal surmounted by a shapeless something swathed in a large sheet—the statue
to Lord Hemel of Hempstead which he had
come down to unveil.

And gradually, as his visit proceeded,
there began to steal over him an emotion
which defied analysis.

At first he supposed it to be a natural
sentimentality. But, had it been that,
would it not have been a more pleasurable
emotion ? For his feelings had begun to be
far from unmixedly agreeable. Once, when
rounding a corner, he came upon the captain
of football in all his majesty, there had swept
over him a hideous blend of fear and shame
which had made his gaitered legs wobble like
jellies. The captain of football doffed his
cap respectfully, and the feeling passed as
quickly as it had come : but not so soon that
the bishop had not recognised it. It was
exactly the feeling he had been wont to have

forty-odd years ago when, sneaking softly away from football practice, he had encountered one in authority.

The bishop was puzzled. It was as if some fairy had touched him with her wand, sweeping away the years and making him an inky-faced boy again. Day by day this illusion grew, the constant society of the Rev. Trevor Entwhistle doing much to foster it. For young Catsmeat Entwhistle had been the bishop's particular crony at Harchester, and he seemed to have altered his appearance since those days in no way whatsoever. The bishop had had a nasty shock when, entering the headmaster's study on the third morning of his visit, he found him sitting in the headmaster's chair with the headmaster's cap and gown on. It had seemed to him that young Catsmeat, in order to indulge his distorted sense of humour, was taking the most frightful risk. Suppose the Old Man were to come in and cop him !

Altogether, it was a relief to the bishop when the day of the unveiling arrived.

The actual ceremony, however, he found both tedious and irritating. Lord Hemel of

Hempstead had not been a favourite of his
in their school days, and there was something
extremely disagreeable to him in being
obliged to roll out sonorous periods in his
praise.

In addition to this, he had suffered from
the very start of the proceedings from a bad
attack of stage fright. He could not help
thinking that he must look the most awful
chump standing up there in front of all those
people and spouting. He half expected one
of the prefects in the audience to step up and
clout his head and tell him not to be a funny
young swine.

However, no disaster of this nature
occurred. Indeed, his speech was notably
successful.

" My dear bishop," said old General
Bloodenough, the Chairman of the College
Board of Governors, shaking his hand at the
conclusion of the unveiling, " your magnificent oration put my own feeble efforts to
shame, put them to shame, to shame. You
were astounding ! "

" Thanks awfully," mumbled the bishop,
blushing and shuffling his feet.

The weariness which had come upon the

bishop as the result of the prolonged ceremony seemed to grow as the day wore on. By the time he was seated in the headmaster's study after dinner he was in the grip of a severe headache.

The Rev. Trevor Entwhistle also appeared jaded.

" These affairs are somewhat fatiguing, bishop," he said, stifling a yawn.

" They are, indeed, Headmaster."

" Even the '87 port seems an inefficient restorative."

" Markedly inefficient. I wonder," said the bishop, struck with an idea, " if a little Buck-U-Uppo might not alleviate our exhaustion. It is a tonic of some kind which my secretary is in the habit of taking. It certainly appears to do him good. A livelier, more vigorous young fellow I have never seen. Suppose we ask your butler to go to his room and borrow the bottle ? I am sure he will be delighted to give it to us."

" By all means."

The butler, dispatched to Augustine's room, returned with a bottle half full of a thick, dark coloured liquid. The bishop examined it thoughtfully.

"I see there are no directions given as to the requisite dose," he said. "However, I do not like to keep disturbing your butler, who has now doubtless returned to his pantry and is once more settling down to the enjoyment of a well-earned rest after a day more than ordinarily fraught with toil and anxiety. Suppose we use our own judgment?"

"Certainly. Is it nasty?"

The bishop licked the cork warily.

"No. I should not call it nasty. The taste, while individual and distinctive and even striking, is by no means disagreeable."

"Then let us take a glassful apiece."

The bishop filled two portly wine-glasses with the fluid, and they sat sipping gravely.

"It's rather good," said the bishop.

"Distinctly good," said the headmaster.

"It sort of sends a kind of glow over you."

"A noticeable glow."

"A little more, Headmaster?"

"No, I thank you."

"Oh, come."

"Well, just a spot, bishop, if you insist."

"It's rather good," said the bishop.

"Distinctly good," said the headmaster.

Now you, who have listened to the story of Augustine's previous adventures with the Buck-U-Uppo, are aware that my brother Wilfred invented it primarily with the object of providing Indian Rajahs with a specific which would encourage their elephants to face the tiger of the jungle with a jaunty sang-froid : and he had advocated as a medium dose for an adult elephant a tea-spoonful stirred up with its morning bran-mash. It is not surprising, therefore, that after they had drunk two wine-glassfuls apiece of the mixture the outlook on life of both the bishop and the headmaster began to undergo a marked change.

Their fatigue had left them, and with it the depression which a few moments before had been weighing on them so heavily. Both were conscious of an extraordinary feeling of good cheer, and the odd illusion of extreme youth which had been upon the bishop since his arrival at Harchester was now more pronounced than ever. He felt a youngish and rather rowdy fifteen.

" Where does your butler sleep, Cats-meat ? " he asked, after a thoughtful pause.

" I don't know. Why ? "

"I was only thinking that it would be a lark to go and put a booby-trap on his door."

The headmaster's eyes glistened.

"Yes, wouldn't it!" he said.

They mused for awhile. Then the headmaster uttered a deep chuckle.

"What are you giggling about?" asked the bishop.

"I was only thinking what a priceless ass you looked this afternoon, talking all that rot about old Fatty."

In spite of his cheerfulness, a frown passed over the bishop's fine forehead.

"It went very much against the grain to speak in terms of eulogy—yes, fulsome eulogy —of one whom we both know to have been a blighter of the worst description. Where does Fatty get off, having statues put up to him?"

"Oh well, he's an Empire builder, I suppose," said the headmaster, who was a fair-minded man.

"Just the sort of thing he would be," grumbled the bishop. "Shoving himself forward! If ever there was a chap I barred, it was Fatty."

" Me, too," agreed the headmaster. " Beastly laugh he'd got. Like glue pouring out of a jug."

" Greedy little beast, if you remember. A fellow in his house told me he once ate three slices of brown boot-polish spread on bread after he had finished the potted meat."

" Between you and me, I always suspected him of swiping buns at the school shop. I don't wish to make rash charges unsupported by true evidence, but it always seemed to me extremely odd that, whatever time of the term it was, and however hard up everybody else might be, you never saw Fatty without his bun."

" Catsmeat," said the bishop, " I'll tell you something about Fatty that isn't generally known. In a scrum in the final House Match in the year 1888 he deliberately hoofed me on the shin."

" You don't mean that ? "

" I do."

" Great Scott ! "

" An ordinary hack on the shin," said the bishop coldly, " no fellow minds. It is part of the give and take of normal social life. But when a bounder deliberately hauls off

and lets drive at you with the sole intention of
laying you out, it—well, it's a bit thick."

"And those chumps of Governors have
put up a statue to him ! "

The bishop leaned forward and lowered
his voice.

" Catsmeat."

" What ? "

" Do you know what ? "

" No, what ? "

" What we ought to do is to wait till
twelve o'clock or so, till there's no one about,
and then beetle out and paint that statue
blue."

" Why not pink ? "

" Pink, if you prefer it."

" Pink's a nice colour."

" It is.   Very nice."

" Besides, I know where I can lay my
hands on some pink paint."

" You do ? "

" Gobs of it."

" Peace be on thy walls, Catsmeat, and
prosperity within thy palaces," said the
bishop.   " Proverbs cxxi. 6."

It seemed to the bishop, as he closed the

front door noiselessly behind him two hours later, that providence, always on the side of the just, was extending itself in its efforts to make this little enterprise of his a success. All the conditions were admirable for statue-painting. The rain which had been falling during the evening had stopped : and a moon, which might have proved an embarrass-ment, was conveniently hidden behind a bank of clouds.

As regarded human interference, they had nothing to alarm them. No place in the world is so deserted as the ground of a school after midnight. Fatty's statue might have been in the middle of the Sahara. They climbed the pedestal, and, taking turns fairly with the brush, soon accomplished the task which their sense of duty had indicated to them. It was only when, treading warily lest their steps should be heard on the gravel drive, they again reached the front door that anything occurred to mar the harmony of the proceedings.

" What are you waiting for ? " whispered the bishop, as his companion lingered on the top step.

" Half a second," said the headmaster

in a muffled voice. " It may be in another
pocket."

" What ? "

" My key."

" Have you lost your key ? "

" I believe I have."

" Catsmeat," said the bishop, with grave
censure, " this is the last time I come out
painting statues with you."

" I must have dropped it somewhere."

" What shall we do ? "

" There's just a chance the scullery
window may be open."

But the scullery window was not open.
Careful, vigilant, and faithful to his trust,
the butler, on retiring to rest, had fastened
it and closed the shutters. They were locked
out.

But it has been well said that it is the
lessons which we learn in our boyhood days
at school that prepare us for the problems of
life in the larger world outside. Stealing
back from the mists of the past, there came
to the bishop a sudden memory.

" Catsmeat ! "

" Hullo ? "

" If you haven't been mucking the place

up with alterations and improvements, there should be a water-pipe round at the back, leading to one of the upstairs windows."

Memory had not played him false. There, nestling in the ivy, was the pipe up and down which he had been wont to climb when, a pie-faced lad in the summer of '86, he had broken out of this house in order to take nocturnal swims in the river.

"Up you go," he said briefly.

The headmaster required no further urging. And presently the two were making good time up the side of the house.

It was just as they reached the window and just after the bishop had informed his old friend that, if he kicked him on the head again, he'd hear of it, that the window was suddenly flung open.

"Who's that?" said a clear young voice.

The headmaster was frankly taken aback. Dim though the light was, he could see that the man leaning out of the window was poising in readiness a very nasty-looking golf-club : and his first impulse was to reveal his identity and so clear himself of the suspicion of being the marauder for whom he gathered the other had mistaken him. Then there presented themselves to him certain objections to revealing his identity, and he hung there in silence, unable to think of a suitable next move.

The bishop was a man of readier resource.

" Tell him we're a couple of cats belonging to the cook," he whispered.

It was painful for one of the headmaster's scrupulous rectitude and honesty to stoop to such a falsehood, but it seemed the only course to pursue.

" It's all right," he said, forcing a note of easy geniality into his voice. " We're a couple of cats."

" Cat-burglars ? "

" No. Just ordinary cats."

" Belonging to the cook," prompted the bishop from below.

" Belonging to the cook," added the headmaster.

" I see," said the man at the window. " Well, in that case, right ho ! "

He stood aside to allow them to enter. The bishop, an artist at heart, mewed gratefully as he passed, to add verisimilitude to the deception : and then made for his bed-

room, accompanied by the headmaster. The
episode was apparently closed.

Nevertheless, the headmaster was dis-
turbed by a certain uneasiness.

"Do you suppose he thought we really
were cats?" he asked anxiously.

"I am not sure," said the bishop.
"But I think we deceived him by the non-
chalance of our demeanour."

"Yes, I think we did. Who was he?"

"My secretary. The young fellow I was
speaking of, who lent us that capital tonic."

"Oh, then that's all right. He wouldn't
give you away."

"No. And there is nothing else that can
possibly lead to our being suspected. We left
no clue whatsoever."

"All the same," said the headmaster
thoughtfully, "I'm beginning to wonder
whether it was in the best sense of the word
judicious to have painted that statue."

"Somebody had to," said the bishop
stoutly.

"Yes, that's true," said the headmaster,
brightening.

The bishop slept late on the following

morning, and partook of his frugal breakfast in bed. The day, which so often brings remorse, brought none to him. Something attempted, something done had earned a night's repose : and he had no regrets— except that, now that it was all over, he was not sure that blue paint would not have been more effective. However, his old friend had pleaded so strongly for the pink that it would have been difficult for himself, as a guest, to override the wishes of his host. Still, blue would undoubtedly have been very striking.

There was a knock on the door, and Augustine entered.

" Morning, Bish."

" Good-morning, Mulliner," said the bishop affably. " I have lain somewhat late to-day."

" I say, Bish," asked Augustine, a little anxiously. " Did you take a very big dose of the Buck-U-Uppo last night ? "

" Big ? No. As I recollect, quite small. Barely two ordinary wine-glasses full."

" Great Scott ! "

" Why do you ask, my dear fellow ? "

" Oh, nothing. No particular reason. I

just thought your manner seemed a little strange on the water-pipe, that's all."

The bishop was conscious of a touch of chagrin.

"Then you saw through our—er—innocent deception?"

"Yes."

"I had been taking a little stroll with the headmaster," explained the bishop, "and he had mislaid his key. How beautiful is Nature at night, Mulliner! The dark, fathomless skies, the little winds that seem to whisper secrets in one's ear, the scent of growing things."

"Yes," said Augustine. He paused. "Rather a row on this morning. Somebody appears to have painted Lord Hemel of Hempstead's statue last night."

"Indeed?"

"Yes."

"Ah, well," said the bishop tolerantly, "boys will be boys."

"It's a most mysterious business."

"No doubt, no doubt. But, after all, Mulliner, is not all Life a mystery?"

"And what makes it still more mysterious is that they found your shovel-hat on the statue's head."

The bishop started up.

" What ! "

" Absolutely."

" Mulliner," said the bishop, " leave me. I have one or two matters on which I wish to meditate."

He dressed hastily, his numbed fingers fumbling with his gaiters. It all came back to him now. Yes, he could remember putting the hat on the statue's head. It had seemed a good thing to do at the time, and he had done it. How little we guess at the moment how far-reaching our most trivial actions may be !

The headmaster was over at the school, instructing the Sixth Form in Greek Composition : and he was obliged to wait, chafing, until twelve-thirty, when the bell rang for the half-way halt in the day's work. He stood at the study window, watching with ill-controlled impatience, and presently the headmaster appeared, walking heavily like one on whose mind there is a weight.

" Well ? " cried the bishop, as he entered the study.

The headmaster doffed his cap and gown, and sank limply into a chair.

" I cannot conceive," he groaned, " what madness had me in its grip last night."

The bishop was shaken, but he could not countenance such an attitude as this.

" I do not understand you, Headmaster," he said stiffly. " It was our simple duty, as a protest against the undue exaltation of one whom we both know to have been a most unpleasant schoolmate, to paint that statue."

" And I suppose it was your duty to leave your hat on its head ? "

" Now there," said the bishop, " I may possibly have gone a little too far." He coughed. " Has that perhaps somewhat ill-considered action led to the harbouring of suspicions by those in authority ? "

" They don't know what to think."

" What is the view of the Board of Governors ? "

" They insist on my finding the culprit. Should I fail to do so, they hint at the gravest consequences."

" You mean they will deprive you of your headmastership ? "

" That is what they imply. I shall be asked to hand in my resignation. And, if

E

that happens, bim goes my chance of ever being a bishop."

" Well, it's not all jam being a bishop. You wouldn't enjoy it, Catsmeat."

" All very well for you to talk, Boko. You got me into this, you silly ass."

" I like that ! You were just as keen on it as I was."

" You suggested it."

" Well, you jumped at the suggestion."

The two men had faced each other heatedly, and for a moment it seemed as if there was to be a serious falling-out. Then the bishop recovered himself.

" Catsmeat," he said, with that wonderful smile of his, taking the other's hand, " this is unworthy of us. We must not quarrel. We must put our heads together and see if there is not some avenue of escape from the unfortunate position in which, however creditable our motives, we appear to have placed ourselves. How would it be——? "

" I thought of that," said the headmaster. " It wouldn't do a bit of good. Of course, we might—— "

" No, that's no use, either," said the bishop.

They sat for awhile in meditative silence. And, as they sat, the door opened.

" General Bloodenough," announced the butler.

" Oh, that I had wings like a dove. Psalm xlv. 6," muttered the bishop.

His desire to be wafted from that spot with all available speed could hardly be considered unreasonable. General Sir Hector Bloodenough, V.C., K.C.I.E., M.V.O., on retiring from the army, had been for many years, until his final return to England, in charge of the Secret Service in Western Africa, where his unerring acumen had won for him from the natives the soubriquet of Wah-nah-B'gosh-B'jingo,—which, freely translated, means Big Chief Who Can See Through The Hole In A Doughnut.

A man impossible to deceive. The last man the bishop would have wished to be conducting the present investigations.

The general stalked into the room. He had keen blue eyes, topped by bushy white eyebrows : and the bishop found his gaze far too piercing to be agreeable.

" Bad business, this," he said. " Bad business. Bad business."

" It is, indeed," faltered the bishop.

" Shocking bad business. Shocking. Shocking. Do you know what we found on the head of that statue, eh ? that statue, that statue ? Your hat, bishop. Your hat. Your hat."

The bishop made an attempt to rally. His mind was in a whirl, for the general's habit of repeating everything three times had the effect on him of making his last night's escapade seem three times as bad. He now saw himself on the verge of standing convicted of having painted three statues with three pots of pink paint, and of having placed on the head of each one of a trio of shovel-hats. But he was a strong man, and he did his best.

" You say my hat ? " he retorted with spirit. " How do you know it was my hat ? There may have been hundreds of bishops dodging about the school grounds last night."

" Got your name in it. Your name. Your name."

The bishop clutched at the arm of the chair in which he sat. The general's eyes were piercing him through and through, and every moment he felt more like a sheep that

has had the misfortune to encounter a potted
meat manufacturer. He was on the point of
protesting that the writing in the hat was
probably a forgery, when there was a tap at
the door.

" Come in," cried the headmaster, who
had been cowering in his seat.

There entered a small boy in an Eton
suit, whose face seemed to the bishop vaguely
familiar. It was a face that closely resembled
a ripe tomato with a nose stuck on it, but
that was not what had struck the bishop.
It was something other than tomatoes that
this lad reminded him.

" Sir, please, sir," said the boy.

" Yes, yes, yes," said General Bloodenough
testily. " Run away, my boy, run away, run
away. Can't you see we're busy ? "

" But, sir, please, sir, it's about the
statue."

" What about the statue ? What about
it ? What about it ? "

" Sir, please, sir, it was me."

" What !   What !   What !   What !
What ! "

The bishop, the general, and the headmaster had spoken simultaneously : and

the "Whats" had been distributed as follows :

The Bishop. 1
The General 3
The Headmaster 1

making five in all. Having uttered these ejaculations, they sat staring at the boy, who turned a brighter vermilion.

" What are you saying ? " cried the headmaster. " You painted that statue ? "

" Sir, yes, sir."

" You ? " said the bishop.

" Sir, yes, sir."

" You ? You ? You ? " said the general.

" Sir, yes, sir."

There was a quivering pause. The bishop looked at the headmaster. The headmaster looked at the bishop. The general looked at the boy. The boy looked at the floor.

The general was the first to speak.

" Monstrous ! " he exclaimed. " Monstrous. Monstrous. Never heard of such a thing. This boy must be expelled, Headmaster. Expelled. Ex—— "

" No ! " said the headmaster in a ringing voice.

" Then flogged within an inch of his life. Within an inch.   An inch."

" No ! "   A strange, new dignity seemed to have descended upon the Rev. Trevor Entwhistle. He was breathing a little quickly through his nose, and his eyes had assumed a somewhat prawn-like aspect.   " In matters of school discipline, general, I must with all deference claim to be paramount.   I will deal with this case as I think best.   In my opinion this is not an occasion for severity.   You agree with me, bishop ? "

The bishop came to himself with a start. He had been thinking of an article which he had just completed for a leading review on the subject of Miracles, and was regretting that the tone he had taken, though in keeping with the trend of Modern Thought, had been tinged with something approaching scepticism.

" Oh, entirely," he said.

" Then all I can say," fumed the general, " is that I wash my hands of the whole business, the whole business, the whole business.   And if this is the way our boys are being brought up nowadays, no wonder the country is going to the dogs, the dogs, going to the dogs."

The door slammed behind him. The headmaster turned to the boy, a kindly, winning smile upon his face.

" No doubt," he said, " you now regret this rash act ? "

" Sir, yes, sir."

" And you would not do it again ? "

" Sir, no, sir."

" Then I think," said the headmaster cheerily, " that we may deal leniently with what, after all, was but a boyish prank, eh, bishop ? "

" Oh, decidedly, Headmaster."

" Quite the sort of thing—ha, ha !— that you or I might have done—er—at his age ? "

" Oh, quite."

" Then you shall write me twenty lines of Virgil, Mulliner, and we will say no more about it."

The bishop sprang from his chair.

" Mulliner ! Did you say Mulliner ? "

" Yes."

" I have a secretary of that name. Are you, by any chance, a relation of his, my lad ? "

" Sir, yes, sir. Brother."

" Oh ! " said the bishop.

The bishop found Augustine in the garden,
squirting whale-oil solution on the rose-
bushes, for he was an enthusiastic horticul-
turist. He placed an affectionate hand on
his shoulder.

" Mulliner," he said, " do not think that
I have not detected your hidden hand
behind this astonishing occurrence."

" Eh ? " said Augustine. " What astonishing occurrence ? "

" As you are aware, Mulliner, last night,
from motives which I can assure you were
honourable and in accord with the truest
spirit of sound Churchmanship, the Rev.
Trevor Entwhistle and I were compelled to
go out and paint old Fatty Hemel's statue
pink. Just now, in the headmaster's study,
a boy confessed that he had done it. That
boy, Mulliner, was your brother."

" Oh yes ? "

" It was you who, in order to save me,
inspired him to that confession. Do not deny
it, Mulliner."

Augustine smiled an embarrassed smile.

" It was nothing, Bish, nothing at all."

" I trust the matter did not involve you in any too great expense. From what I know of brothers, the lad was scarcely likely to have carried through this benevolent ruse for nothing."

" Oh, just a couple of quid. He wanted three, but I beat him down. Preposterous, I mean to say," said Augustine warmly. " Three quid for a perfectly simple, easy job like that ? And so I told him."

" It shall be returned to you, Mulliner."

" No, no, Bish."

" Yes, Mulliner, it shall be returned to you. I have not the sum on my person, but I will forward you a cheque to your new address, The Vicarage, Steeple Mummery, Hants."

Augustine's eyes filled with sudden tears. He grasped the other's hand.

" Bish," he said in a choking voice, " I don't know how to thank you. But—have you considered ? "

" Considered ? "

" The wife of thy bosom. Deuteronomy xiii. 6. What will she say when you tell her ? "

The bishop's eyes gleamed with a resolute light.

" Mulliner," he said, " the point you raise had not escaped me. But I have the situation well in hand. A bird of the air shall carry the voice, and that which hath wings shall tell the matter. Ecclesiastes x. 20. I shall inform her of my decision on the long-distance telephone."

V

CAME THE DAWN

THE man in the corner took a sip of stout-and-mild, and proceeded to point the moral of the story which he had just told us.

"Yes, gentlemen," he said, "Shakespeare was right. There's a divinity that shapes our ends, rough-hew them how we will."

We nodded. He had been speaking of a favourite dog of his which, entered recently by some error in a local cat show, had taken first prize in the class for short-haired tortoiseshells; and we all thought the quotation well-chosen and apposite.

"There is, indeed," said Mr. Mulliner. "A rather similar thing happened to my nephew Lancelot."

In the nightly reunions in the bar-parlour

of the Anglers' Rest we have been trained to believe almost anything of Mr. Mulliner's relatives, but this, we felt, was a little too much.

" You mean to say your nephew Lancelot took a prize at a cat show ? "

" No, no," said Mr. Mulliner hastily. " Certainly not. I have never deviated from the truth in my life, and I hope I never shall. No Mulliner has ever taken a prize at a cat show. No Mulliner, indeed, to the best of my knowledge, has even been entered for such a competition. What I meant was that the fact that we never know what the future holds in store for us was well exemplified in the case of my nephew Lancelot, just as it was in the case of this gentleman's dog which suddenly found itself transformed for all practical purposes into a short-haired tortoiseshell cat. It is rather a curious story, and provides a good illustration of the adage that you never can tell and that it is always darkest before the dawn."

At the time at which my story opens (said Mr. Mulliner) Lancelot, then twenty-four years of age and recently come down from

Oxford, was spending a few days with old Jeremiah Briggs, the founder and proprietor of the famous Briggs's Breakfast Pickles, on the latter's yacht at Cowes.

This Jeremiah Briggs was Lancelot's uncle on the mother's side, and he had always interested himself in the boy. It was he who had sent him to the University; and it was the great wish of his heart that his nephew, on completing his education, should join him in the business. It was consequently a shock to the poor old gentleman when, as they sat together on deck on the first morning of the visit, Lancelot, while expressing the greatest respect for pickles as a class, firmly refused to start in and learn the business from the bottom up.

" The fact is, uncle," he said, " I have mapped out a career for myself on far different lines. I am a poet."

" A poet ? When did you feel this coming on ? "

" Shortly after my twenty-second birthday."

" Well," said the old man, overcoming his first natural feeling of repulsion, " I don't see why that should stop us getting together. I use quite a lot of poetry in my business."

" I fear I could not bring myself to commercialise my Muse."

" Young man," said Mr. Briggs, " if an onion with a head like yours came into my factory, I would refuse to pickle it."

He stumped below, thoroughly incensed. But Lancelot merely uttered a light laugh. He was young; it was summer; the sky was blue; the sun was shining; and the things in the world that really mattered were not cucumbers and vinegar but Romance and Love. Oh, he felt, for some delightful girl to come along on whom he might lavish all the pent-up fervour which had been sizzling inside him for weeks!

And at this moment he saw her.

She was leaning against the rail of a yacht that lay at its moorings some forty yards away; and, as he beheld her, Lancelot's heart leaped like a young gherkin in the boiling-vat. In her face, it seemed to him, was concentrated all the beauty of all the ages. Confronted with this girl, Cleopatra would have looked like Nellie Wallace, and Helen of Troy might have been her plain

sister. He was still gazing at her in a sort
of trance, when the bell sounded for luncheon
and he had to go below.

All through the meal, while his uncle spoke
of pickled walnuts he had known, Lancelot
remained in a reverie. He was counting the
minutes until he could get on deck and start
goggling again. Judge, therefore, of his dis-
may when, on bounding up the companion-
way, he found that the other yacht had disappeared. He recalled now having heard a
sort of harsh, grating noise towards the end
of luncheon ; but at the time he had merely
thought it was his uncle eating celery. Too
late he realised that it must have been the
raising of the anchor-chain.

Although at heart a dreamer, Lancelot
Mulliner was not without a certain practical
streak. Thinking the matter over, he soon
hit upon a rough plan of action for getting
on the track of the fair unknown who had
flashed in and out of his life with such tragic
abruptness. A girl like that—beautiful, lissom, and—as far as he had been able to tell
at such long range—gimp, was sure to be
fond of dancing. The chances were, there-

fore, that sooner or later he would find her at some night club or other.

He started, accordingly, to make the round of the night clubs. As soon as one was raided, he went on to another. Within a month he had visited the Mauve Mouse, the Scarlet Centipede, the Vicious Cheese, the Gay Fritter, the Placid Prune, the Café de Bologna, Billy's, Milly's, Ike's, Spike's, Mike's, and the Ham and Beef. And it was at the Ham and Beef that at last he found her.

He had gone there one evening for the fifth time, principally because at that establishment there were a couple of speciality dancers to whom he had taken a dislike shared by virtually every thinking man in London. It had always seemed to him that one of these nights the male member of the team, while whirling his partner round in a circle by her outstretched arms, might let her go and break her neck ; and though constant disappointment had to some extent blunted the first fine enthusiasm of his early visits, he still hoped.

On this occasion the speciality dancers came and went unscathed as usual, but Lancelot hardly noticed them. His whole attention was concentrated on the girl seated across the room immediately opposite him. It was beyond a question she.

Well, you know what poets are. When their emotions are stirred, they are not like us dull, diffident fellows. They breathe quickly through their noses and get off to a flying start. In one bound Lancelot was across the room, his heart beating till it sounded like a by-request solo from the trap-drummer.

" Shall we dance ? " he said.

" Can you dance ? " said the girl.

Lancelot gave a short, amused laugh. He had had a good University education, and had not failed to profit by it. He was a man who never let his left hip know what his right hip was doing.

" I am old Colonel Charleston's favourite son," he said, simply.

A sound like the sudden descent of an iron girder on a sheet of tin, followed by a jangling of bells, a wailing of tortured cats, and the noise of a few steam-riveters at work, announced to their trained ears that the music had begun. Sweeping her to him with a violence which, attempted in any other place, would have earned him a sentence of thirty days coupled with some strong remarks from the Bench, Lancelot began to push her yielding form through the sea of humanity till they reached the centre of the whirlpool. There, unable to move in any direction, they surrendered themselves to the ecstasy of the dance, wiping their feet on the polished flooring and occasionally pushing an elbow into some stranger's encroaching rib.

" This," murmured the girl with closed eyes, " is divine."

" What ? " bellowed Lancelot, for the orchestra, in addition to ringing bells, had now begun to howl like wolves at dinner-time.

" Divine," roared the girl. " You certainly are a beautiful dancer."

" A beautiful what ? "

" Dancer."

" Who is ? "

" You are."

" Good egg ! " shrieked Lancelot, rather wishing, though he was fond of music, that the orchestra would stop beating the floor with hammers.

" What did you say ? "

" I said, ' Good egg.' "

" Why ? "

" Because the idea crossed my mind that, if you felt like that, you might care to marry me."

There was a sudden lull in the storm. It was as if the audacity of his words had stricken the orchestra into a sort of paralysis. Dark-complexioned men who had been exploding bombs and touching off automobile hooters became abruptly immobile and sat rolling their eyeballs. One or two people left the floor, and plaster stopped falling from the ceiling.

" Marry you ? " said the girl.

" I love you as no man has ever loved woman before."

" Well, that's always something. What would the name be ? "

" Mulliner. Lancelot Mulliner."

" It might be worse." She looked at him with pensive eyes. " Well, why not ? " she said. " It would be a crime to let a dancer like you go out of the family. On the other hand, my father will kick like a mule. Father is an Earl."

" What Earl ? "

" The Earl of Biddlecombe."

"Well, earls aren't everything," said Lancelot with a touch of pique. "The Mulliners are an old and honourable family. A Sieur de Moulinières came over with the Conqueror."

"Ah, but did a Sieur de Moulinières ever do down the common people for a few hundred thousand and salt it away in gilt-edged securities? That's what's going to count with the aged parent. What with taxes and super-taxes and death duties and falling land-values, there has of recent years been very, very little of the right stuff in the Biddlecombe sock. Shake the family money-box and you will hear but the faintest rattle. And I ought to tell you that at the Junior Lipstick Club seven to two is being freely offered on my marrying Slingsby Purvis, of Purvis's Liquid Dinner Glue. Nothing is definitely decided yet, but you can take it as coming straight from the stable that, unless something happens to upset current form, she whom you now see before you is the future Ma Purvis."

Lancelot stamped his foot defiantly, eliciting a howl of agony from a passing reveller.

"This shall not be," he muttered.

" If you care to bet against it," said the
girl, producing a small note-book, " I can
accommodate you at the current odds."

" Purvis, forsooth ! "

" I'm not saying it's a pretty name. All
I'm trying to point out is that at the present
moment he heads the ' All the above have
arrived ' list. He is Our Newmarket Cor-
respondent's Five-Pound Special and Captain
Coe's final selection. What makes you think
you can nose him out ? Are you rich ? "

" At   present,   only   in   love.   But   to-
morrow I go to my uncle, who is immensely
wealthy—— "

" And touch him ? "

" Not quite that. Nobody has touched
Uncle Jeremiah since the early winter of 1885.
But I shall get him to give me a job, and then
we shall see."

" Do," said the girl, warmly. " And if
you can stick the gaff into Purvis and work
the Young Lochinvar business, I shall be the
first to touch off red fire. On the other hand,
it is only fair to inform you that at the
Junior Lipstick all the girls look on the race
as a walk-over. None of the big punters will
touch it."

Lancelot returned to his rooms that night undiscouraged. He intended to sink his former prejudices and write a poem in praise of Briggs's Breakfast Pickles which would mark a new era in commercial verse. This he would submit to his uncle ; and, having stunned him with it, would agree to join the firm as chief poetry-writer. He tentatively pencilled down five thousand pounds a year as the salary which he would demand. With a long-term contract for five thousand a year in his pocket, he could approach Lord Biddle-combe and jerk a father's blessing out of him in no time. It would be humiliating, of course, to lower his genius by writing poetry about pickles ; but a lover must make sacrifices. He bought a quire of the best foolscap, brewed a quart of the strongest coffee, locked his door, disconnected his telephone, and sat down at his desk.

Genial old Jeremiah Briggs received him, when he called next day at his palatial house, the Villa Chutney, at Putney, with a bluff good-humour which showed that he still had a warm spot in his heart for the young rascal.

" Sit down, boy, and have a pickled

onion," said he, cheerily, slapping Lancelot
on the shoulder. " You've come to tell me
you've reconsidered your idiotic decision
about not joining the business, eh ? No
doubt we thought it a little beneath our
dignity to start at the bottom and work our
way up ? But, consider, my dear lad. We
must learn to walk before we can run, and
you could hardly expect me to make you
chief cucumber-buyer, or head of the vine-
gar-bottling department, before you have
acquired hard-won experience."

" If you will allow me to explain, uncle
———"

" Eh ? " Mr. Briggs's geniality faded
somewhat. " Am I to understand that you
don't want to come into the business ? "

" Yes and no," said Lancelot. " I still
consider that slicing up cucumbers and dipping them in vinegar is a poor life-work for
a man with the Promethean fire within him ;
but I propose to place at the disposal of the
Briggs Breakfast Pickle my poetic gifts."

" Well, that's better than nothing. I've
just been correcting the proofs of the last
thing our man turned in. It's really excellent. Listen :

" *Soon, soon all human joys must end :*
Grim Death approaches with his sickle :
Courage ! There is still time, my friend,
To eat a Briggs's Breakfast Pickle."

" If you could give us something like that—— "

Lancelot raised his eyebrows. His lip curled.

" The little thing I have dashed off is not quite like that."

" Oh, you've written something, eh ? "

" A mere *morceau*. You would care to hear it ? "

" Fire away, my boy."

Lancelot produced his manuscript and cleared his throat. He began to read in a low, musical voice.

" DARKLING (A Threnody).

By L. Bassington Mulliner.

(*Copyright in all languages, including the Scandinavian.*)

(*The dramatic, musical comedy, and motion picture rights of this Threnody are strictly reserved. Applications for these should be made to the author.*) "

"What is a Threnody?" asked Mr. Briggs.

"This is," said Lancelot.

He cleared his throat again and resumed.

"*Black branches,*
Like a corpse's withered hands,
Waving against the blacker sky :
Chill winds,
Bitter like the tang of half-remembered sins ;
Bats wheeling mournfully through the air,
And on the ground
Worms,
Toads,
Frogs,
And nameless creeping things ;
And all around
Desolation,
Doom,
Dyspepsia,
And Despair.
I am a bat that wheels through the air of
    Fate ;
I am a worm that wriggles in a swamp of
    Disillusionment ;
I am a despairing toad ;
I have got dyspepsia."

He paused. His uncle's eyes were protruding rather like those of a nameless creeping frog.

" What's all this ? " said Mr. Briggs.

It seemed almost incredible to Lancelot that his poem should present any aspect of obscurity to even the meanest intellect ; but he explained.

" The thing," he said, " is symbolic. It essays to depict the state of mind of the man who has not yet tried Briggs's Breakfast Pickles. I shall require it to be printed in hand-set type on deep cream-coloured paper."

" Yes ? " said Mr. Briggs, touching the bell.

" With bevelled edges. It must be published, of course, bound in limp leather, preferably of a violet shade, in a limited edition, confined to one hundred and five copies. Each of these copies I will sign—— "

" You rang, sir ? " said the butler, appearing in the doorway.

Mr. Briggs nodded curtly.

" Bewstridge," said he, " throw Mr. Lancelot out."

" Very good, sir."

" And see," added Mr. Briggs, superintending the subsequent proceedings from his library window, " that he never darkens my

doors again.   When you have finished, Bewstridge, ring up my lawyers on the telephone.
I wish to alter my will."

Youth is a resilient period.   With all his
worldly prospects swept away and a large
bruise on his person which made it uncom-
fortable for him to assume a sitting posture,
you might have supposed that the return
of Lancelot Mulliner from Putney would have
resembled that of the late Napoleon from
Moscow.   Such, however, was not the case.
What, Lancelot asked himself as he rode back
to civilisation on top of an omnibus, did
money matter ?   Love, true love, was all.
He would go to Lord Biddlecombe and tell
him so in a few neatly-chosen words.   And
his lordship, moved by his eloquence, would
doubtless drop a well-bred tear and at once
see that the arrangements for his wedding to
Angela—for such, he had learned, was her
name—were hastened along with all possible
speed.   So uplifted was he by this picture
that he began to sing, and would have continued for the remainder of the journey had
not the conductor in a rather brusque manner
ordered him to desist.   He was obliged to

content himself until the bus reached Hyde Park Corner by singing in dumb show.

The Earl of Biddlecombe's town residence was in Berkeley Square. Lancelot rang the bell and a massive butler appeared.

" No hawkers, street criers, or circulars," said the butler.

" I wish to see Lord Biddlecombe."

" Is his lordship expecting you ? "

" Yes," said Lancelot, feeling sure that the girl would have spoken to her father over the morning toast and marmalade of a possible visit from him.

A voice made itself heard through an open door on the left of the long hall.

" Fotheringay."

" Your lordship ? "

" Is that the feller ? "

" Yes, your lordship."

" Then bung him in, Fotheringay."

" Very good, your lordship."

Lancelot found himself in a small, comfortably-furnished room, confronting a dignified-looking old man with a patrician nose and small side-whiskers, who looked like something that long ago had come out of an egg.

" Afternoon," said this individual.

" Good afternoon, Lord Biddlecombe,"
said Lancelot.

" Now, about these trousers."

" I beg your pardon ? "

" These trousers," said the other, extending a shapely leg. " Do they fit ? Aren't
they a bit baggy round the ankles ? Won't
they jeopardise my social prestige if I am
seen in them in the Park ? "

Lancelot was charmed with his affability.
It gave him the feeling of having been made
one of the family straight away.

" You really want my opinion ? "

" I do. I want your candid opinion as a
God-fearing man and a member of a West-
end tailoring firm."

" But I'm not."

" Not a God-fearing man ? "

"Not a member of a West-end tailoring
firm."

" Come, come," said his lordship, testily.
" You represent Gusset and Mainprice, of
Cork Street."

" No, I don't."

" Then who the devil are you ? "

" My name is Mulliner."

Lord Biddlecombe rang the bell furiously.

" Fotheringay ! "

" Your lordship ? "

" You told me this man was the feller I was expecting from Gusset and Mainprice."

" He certainly led me to suppose so, your lordship."

" Well, he isn't. His name is Mulliner. And—this is the point, Fotheringay. This is the core and centre of the thing—what the blazes does he want ? "

" I could not say, your lordship."

" I came here, Lord Biddlecombe," said Lancelot, " to ask your consent to my immediate marriage with your daughter."

" My daughter ? "

" Your daughter."

" Which daughter ? "

" Angela."

" My daughter Angela ? "

" Yes."

" You want to marry my daughter Angela ? "

" I do."

" Oh ? Well, be that as it may," said Lord Biddlecombe, " can I interest you in an ingenious little combination mousetrap and pencil-sharpener ? "

Lancelot was for a moment a little taken aback by the question. Then, remembering what Angela had said of the state of the family finances, he recovered his poise. He thought no worse of this Grecian-beaked old man for ekeing out a slender income by acting as agent for the curious little object which he was now holding out to him. Many of the aristocracy, he was aware, had been forced into similar commercial enterprises by recent legislation of a harsh and Socialistic trend.

" I should like it above all things," he said, courteously. " I was thinking only this morning that it was just what I needed."

" Highly educational. Not a toy. Fotheringay, book one Mouso-Penso."

" Very good, your lordship."

" Are you troubled at all with headaches, Mr. Mulliner ? "

" Very seldom."

" Then what you want is Clark's Cure for Corns. Shall we say one of the large bottles ? "

" Certainly."

" Then that—with a year's subscription to ' Our Tots '—will come to precisely one pound three shillings and sixpence. Thank you. Will there be anything further ? "

" No, thank you. Now, touching the matter of——— "

" You wouldn't care for a scarf-pin ? Any ties, collars, shirts ? No ? Then good-bye, Mr. Mulliner."

" But——— "

" Fotheringay," said Lord Biddlecombe, " throw Mr. Mulliner out."

As Lancelot scrambled to his feet from the hard pavement of Berkeley Square, he was conscious of a rush of violent anger which deprived him momentarily of speech. He stood there, glaring at the house from which he had been ejected, his face working hideously. So absorbed was he that it was some time before he became aware that somebody was plucking at his coat-sleeve.

" Pardon me, sir."

Lancelot looked round. A stout smooth-faced man with horn-rimmed spectacles was standing beside him.

" If you could spare me a moment——— "

Lancelot shook him off impatiently. He had no desire at a time like this to chatter with strangers. The man was babbling

F

something, but the words made no impression upon his mind. With a savage scowl, Lancelot snatched the fellow's umbrella from him and, poising it for an instant, flung it with a sure aim through Lord Biddlecombe's study window. Then, striding away, he made for Berkeley Street. Glancing over his shoulder as he turned the corner, he saw that Fotheringay, the butler, had come out of the house and was standing over the spectacled man with a certain quiet menace in his demeanour. He was rolling up his sleeves, and his fingers were twitching a little.

Lancelot dismissed the man from his thoughts. His whole mind now was concentrated on the coming interview with Angela. For he had decided that the only thing to do was to seek her out at her club, where she would doubtless be spending the afternoon, and plead with her to follow the dictates of her heart and, abandoning parents and wealthy suitors, come with her true mate to a life of honest poverty sweetened by love and *vers libre*.

Arriving at the Junior Lipstick, he inquired for her, and the hall-porter dispatched a boy in buttons to fetch her from the billiard-room, where she was refereeing the finals of the Débutantes' Shove-Ha'penny Tournament. And presently his heart leaped as he saw her coming towards him, looking more like a vision of Springtime than anything human and earthly. She was smoking a cigarette in a long holder, and as she approached she inserted a monocle inquiringly in her right eye.

" Hullo, laddie ! " she said. " You here ? What's on the mind besides hair ? Talk quick. I've only got a minute."

" Angela," said Lancelot, " I have to report a slight hitch in the programme which I sketched out at our last meeting. I have just been to see my uncle and he has washed his hands of me and cut me out of his will."

" Nothing doing in that quarter, you mean ? " said the girl, chewing her lower lip thoughtfully.

" Nothing. But what of it ? What matters it so long as we have each other ? Money is dross. Love is everything. Yes, love indeed is light from heaven, a spark of that immortal fire with angels shared, by Allah given to lift from earth our low desire.

Give me to live with Love alone, and let the
world go dine and dress. If life's a flower,
I choose my own. 'Tis Love in Idleness.
When beauty fires the blood, how love
exalts the mind! Come, Angela, let us
read together in a book more moving than the
Koran, more eloquent than Shakespeare, the
book of books, the crown of all literature—
Bradshaw's Railway Guide. We will turn
up a page and you shall put your finger down,
and wherever it rests there we will go, to
live for ever with our happiness. Oh, Angela,
let us—— "

" Sorry," said the girl. " Purvis wins.
The race goes by the form-book after all.
There was a time when I thought you might
be going to crowd him on the rails and get
your nose first under the wire with a quick
last-minute dash, but apparently it is not to
be. Deepest sympathy, old crocus, but that's
that."

Lancelot staggered.

" You mean you intend to marry this
Purvis ? "

" Pop in about a month from now at
St. George's, Hanover Square, and see for
yourself."

" You would allow this man to buy you
with his gold ? "

" Don't overlook his diamonds."

" Does love count for nothing ? Surely
you love me ? "

" Of course I do, my desert king. When
you do that flat-footed Black Bottom step
with the sort of wiggly twiggle at the end,
I feel as if I were eating plovers' eggs in a
new dress to the accompaniment of heavenly
music." She sighed. " Yes, I love you,
Lancelot. And women are not like men.
They do not love lightly. When a woman
gives her heart, it is for ever. The years
will pass, and you will turn to another.
But I shall not forget. However, as you
haven't a bob in the world——" She
beckoned to the hall-porter. " Margerison."

" Your ladyship ? "

" Is it raining ? "

" No, your ladyship."

" Are the front steps clean ? "

" Yes, your ladyship."

" Then throw Mr. Mulliner out."

Lancelot leaned against the railings of the
Junior Lipstick, and looked out through a
black mist upon a world that heaved and

rocked and seemed on the point of disinte-grating into ruin and chaos. And a lot he would care, he told himself bitterly, if it did. If Seamore Place from the west and Charles Street from the east had taken a running jump and landed on the back of his neck, it would have added little or nothing to the turmoil of his mind. In fact, he would rather have preferred it.

Fury, as it had done on the pavement of Berkeley Square, robbed him of speech. But his hands, his shoulders, his brows, his lips, his nose, and even his eyelashes seemed to be charged with a silent eloquence. He twitched his eyebrows in agony. He twiddled his fingers in despair. Nothing was left now, he felt, as he shifted the lobe of his left ear in a nor'-nor'-easterly direction, but suicide. Yes, he told him-self, tightening and relaxing the muscles of his cheeks, all that remained now was death.

But, even as he reached this awful decision, a kindly voice spoke in his ear.

"Oh, come now, I wouldn't say that," said the kindly voice.

And Lancelot, turning, perceived the

smooth-faced man who had tried to engage him in conversation in Berkeley Square.

"Say, listen," said the smooth-faced man, sympathy in each lens of his horn-rimmed spectacles. "Tempests may lower and a strong man stand face to face with his soul, but hope, like a healing herb, will show the silver lining where beckons joy and life and happiness."

Lancelot eyed him haughtily.

"I am not aware—— " he began.

"Say, listen," said the other, laying a soothing hand on his shoulder. "I know just what has happened. Mammon has conquered Cupid, and once more youth has had to learn the old, old lesson that though the face be fair the heart may be cold and callous."

"What—— ? "

The smooth-faced man raised his hand.

"That afternoon. Her apartment. 'No. It can never be. I shall wed a wealthier wooer.' "

Lancelot's fury began to dissolve into awe. There seemed something uncanny in the way this total stranger had diagnosed the situation. He stared at him, bewildered.

" How did you know ? " he gasped.

" You told me."

" I ? "

" Your face did. I could read every word. I've been watching you for the last two minutes, and, say, boy, it was a wow ! "

" Who are you ? " asked Lancelot.

The smooth-faced man produced from his waistcoat pocket a fountain-pen, two cigars, a packet of chewing-gum, a small button bearing the legend, " Boost for Hollywood," and a visiting-card—in the order named. Replacing the other articles, he handed the card to Lancelot.

" I'm Isadore Zinzinheimer, kid," he said. " I represent the Bigger, Better, and Brighter Motion-Picture Company of Hollywood, Cal., incorporated last July for sixteen hundred million dollars. And if you're thinking of asking me what I want, I want you. Yes, sir ! Say, listen. A fellow that can register the way you can is needed in my business ; and, if you think money can stop me getting him, name the biggest salary you can think of and hear me laugh. Boy, I use bank-notes for summer underclothing, and I don't care how bad you've got the gimme's if only you'll sign on the dotted line. Say, listen. A bozo that with a mere twitch of the upper lip can make it plain to one and all that he loves a haughty aristocrat and that she has given him the air because his rich uncle, who is a pickle manufacturer living in Putney, won't have anything more to do with him, is required out at Hollywood by the next boat if the movies are ever to become an educational force in the truest and deepest sense of the words."

Lancelot stared at him.

" You want me to come to Hollywood ? "

" I want you, and I'm going to get you. And if you think you're going to prevent me, you're trying to stop Niagara with a tennis racket. Boy, you're great ! When you register, you register. Your face is as chatty as a board of directors. Say, listen. You know the great thing we folks in the motion-picture industry have got to contend with ? The curse of the motion-picture industry is that in every audience there are from six to seven young women with adenoids who will insist on reading out the titles as they are flashed on the screen, filling the rest of the customers with harsh thoughts and dreams of murder. What we're trying to collect is stars that can register so well that titles won't be needed. And, boy, you're the king of them. I know you're feeling good and sore just now because that beazle in there spurned your honest love ; but forget it. Think of your Art. Think of your Public. Come now, what shall we say to start with ? Five thousand a week ? Ten thousand ? You call the shots, and I'll provide the blank contract and fountain-pen."

Lancelot needed no further urging. Already love had turned to hate, and he no longer wished to marry Angela. Instead, he wanted to make her burn with anguish and vain regrets ; and it seemed to him that Fate was pointing the way. Pretty silly the future Lady Angela Purvis would feel when she discovered that she had rejected the love of a man with a salary of ten thousand dollars a week. And fairly foolish her old father would feel when news reached him of the good thing he had allowed to get away. And racking would be the remorse, when he returned to London as Civilised Girlhood's Sweetheart and they saw him addressing mobs from a hotel balcony, of his Uncle Jeremiah, of Fotheringay, of Bewstridge, and of Margerison.

A light gleamed in Lancelot's eye, and he rolled the tip of his nose in a circular movement.

" You consent ? " said Mr. Zinzinheimer, delighted. " 'At-a-boy ! Here's the pen and here's the contract."

" Gimme ! " said Lancelot.

A benevolent glow irradiated the other's spectacles.

" Came the Dawn ! " he murmured. " Came the Dawn ! "

VI

THE STORY OF WILLIAM

MISS POSTLETHWAITE, our able and vigilant barmaid, had whispered to us that the gentleman sitting over there in the corner was an American gentleman.

"Comes from America," added Miss Postlethwaite, making her meaning clearer.

"From America?" echoed we.

"From America," said Miss Postlethwaite. "He's an American."

Mr. Mulliner rose with an old-world grace. We do not often get Americans in the bar-parlour of the Anglers' Rest. When we do, we welcome them. We make them realise that Hands Across the Sea is no mere phrase.

"Good evening, sir," said Mr. Mulliner. "I wonder if you would care to join my friend and myself in a little refreshment?"

"Very kind of you, sir."

" Miss Postlethwaite, the usual. I understand you are from the other side, sir. Do
you find our English country-side pleasant ? "

" Delightful. Though, of course, if I may
say so, scarcely to be compared with the
scenery of my home State."

" What State is that ? "

" California," replied the other, baring
his head. " California, the Jewel State of
the Union. With its azure sea, its noble
hills, its eternal sunshine, and its fragrant
flowers, California stands alone. Peopled by
stalwart men and womanly women . . ."

" California would be all right," said Mr.
Mulliner, " if it wasn't for the earthquakes."

Our guest started as though some veno-
mous snake had bitten him.

" Earthquakes are absolutely unknown in
California," he said, hoarsely.

" What about the one in 1906 ? "

" That was not an earthquake. It was a
fire."

" An earthquake, I always understood,"
said Mr. Mulliner. " My Uncle William was
out there during it, and many a time has he
said to me, ' My boy, it was the San Francisco
earthquake that won me a bride.' "

.

" Couldn't have been the earthquake. May have been the fire."

" Well, I will tell you the story, and you shall judge for yourself."

" I shall be glad to hear your story about the San Francisco fire," said the Californian, courteously.

My Uncle William (said Mr. Mulliner) was returning from the East at the time. The commercial interests of the Mulliners have always been far-flung : and he had been over in China looking into the workings of a tea-exporting business in which he held a number of shares. It was his intention to get off the boat at San Francisco and cross the continent by rail. He particularly wanted to see the Grand Canyon of Arizona. And when he found that Myrtle Banks had for years cherished the same desire, it seemed to him so plain a proof that they were twin souls that he decided to offer her his hand and heart without delay.

This Miss Banks had been a fellow-traveller on the boat all the way from Hong-Kong ; and day by day William Mulliner had fallen more and more deeply in love with her. So on the last day of the voyage, as they were steaming in at the Golden Gate, he proposed.

I have never been informed of the exact words which he employed, but no doubt they were eloquent. All the Mulliners have been able speakers, and on such an occasion, he would, of course, have extended himself. When at length he finished, it seemed to him that the girl's attitude was distinctly promising. She stood gazing over the rail into the water below in a sort of rapt way. Then she turned.

" Mr. Mulliner," she said, " I am greatly flattered and honoured by what you have just told me." These things happened, you will remember, in the days when girls talked like that. " You have paid me the greatest compliment a man can bestow on a woman. And yet . . ."

William Mulliner's heart stood still. He did not like that " And yet—— "

" Is there another ? " he muttered.

" Well, yes, there is. Mr. Franklyn proposed to me this morning. I told him I would think it over."

There was a silence. William was telling

himself that he had been afraid of that bounder Franklyn all along. He might have known, he felt, that Desmond Franklyn would be a menace. The man was one of those lean, keen, hawk-faced, Empire-building sort of chaps you find out East—the kind of fellow who stands on deck chewing his moustache with a far-away look in his eyes, and then, when the girl asks him what he is thinking about, draws a short, quick breath and says he is sorry to be so absent-minded, but a sunset like that always reminds him of the day when he killed the four pirates with his bare hands and saved dear old Tuppy Smithers in the nick of time.

"There is a great glamour about Mr. Franklyn," said Myrtle Banks. "We women admire men who do things. A girl cannot help but respect a man who once killed three sharks with a Boy Scout pocket-knife."

"So he says," growled William.

"He showed me the pocket-knife," said the girl, simply. "And on another occasion he brought down two lions with one shot."

William Mulliner's heart was heavy, but he struggled on.

"Very possibly he may have done these

things," he said, " but surely marriage means more than this. Personally, if I were a girl, I would go rather for a certain steadiness and stability of character. To illustrate what I mean, did you happen to see me win the Egg-and-Spoon race at the ship's sports ? Now there, it seems to me, in what I might call microcosm, was an exhibition of all the qualities a married man most requires—intense coolness, iron resolution, and a quiet, unassuming courage. The man who under test conditions has carried an egg once and a half times round a deck in a small spoon, is a man who can be trusted."

She seemed to waver, but only for a moment.

" I must think," she said. " I must think."

" Certainly," said William. " You will let me see something of you at the hotel, after we have landed ? "

" Of course. And if—I mean to say, whatever happens, I shall always look on you as a dear, dear friend."

" M'yes," said William Mulliner.

For three days my Uncle William's stay

in San Francisco was as pleasant as could reasonably be expected, considering that Desmond Franklyn was also stopping at his and Miss Banks's hotel. He contrived to get the girl to himself to quite a satisfactory extent ; and they spent many happy hours together in the Golden Gate Park and at the Cliff House, watching the seals basking on the rocks. But on the evening of the third day the blow fell.

" Mr. Mulliner," said Myrtle Banks, " I want to tell you something."

" Anything," breathed William tenderly, " except that you are going to marry that perisher Franklyn."

" But that is exactly what I was going to tell you, and I must not let you call him a perisher, for he is a very brave, intrepid man."

" When did you decide on this rash act ? " asked William dully.

" Scarcely an hour ago. We were talking in the garden, and somehow or other we got on to the subject of rhinoceroses. He then told me how he had once been chased up a tree by a rhinoceros in Africa and escaped by throwing pepper in the brute's eyes. He most fortunately chanced to be eating his lunch when the animal arrived, and he had a hard-boiled egg and the pepper-pot in his hands. When I heard this story, like Desdemona, I loved him for the dangers he had passed, and he loved me that I did pity them. The wedding is to be in June."

William Mulliner ground his teeth in a sudden access of jealous rage.

" Personally," he said, " I consider that the story you have just related reveals this man Franklyn in a very dubious—I might almost say sinister—light. On his own showing, the leading trait in his character appears to be cruelty to animals. The fellow seems totally incapable of meeting a shark or a rhinoceros or any other of our dumb friends without instantly going out of his way to inflict bodily injury on it. The last thing I would wish is to be indelicate, but I cannot refrain from pointing out that, if your union is blessed, your children will probably be the sort of children who kick cats and tie tin cans to dogs' tails. If you take my advice, you will write the man a little note, saying that you are sorry but you have changed your mind."

The girl rose in a marked manner.

"I do not require your advice, Mr. Mulliner," she said, coldly. "And I have not changed my mind."

Instantly William Mulliner was all contrition. There is a certain stage in the progress of a man's love when he feels like curling up in a ball and making little bleating noises if the object of his affections so much as looks squiggle-eyed at him ; and this stage my Uncle William had reached. He followed her as she paced proudly away through the hotel lobby, and stammered incoherent apologies. But Myrtle Banks was adamant.

"Leave me, Mr. Mulliner," she said, pointing at the revolving door that led into the street. "You have maligned a better man than yourself, and I wish to have nothing more to do with you. Go ! "

William went, as directed. And so great was the confusion of his mind that he got stuck in the revolving door and had gone round in it no fewer than eleven times before the hall-porter came to extricate him.

"I would have removed you from the machinery earlier, sir," said the hall-porter deferentially, having deposited him safely

in the street, " but my bet with my mate
in there called for ten laps. I waited till you
had completed eleven so that there should be
no argument."

William looked at him dazedly.

" Hall-porter," he said.

" Sir ? "

" Tell me, hall-porter," said William,
" suppose the only girl you have ever loved
had gone and got engaged to another, what
would you do ? "

The hall-porter considered.

" Let me get this right," he said.   " The
proposition is, if I have followed you correctly,
what would I do supposing the Jane on whom
I had always looked as a steady mamma had
handed me the old skimmer and told me to
take all the air I needed because she had
gotten another sweetie ? "

" Precisely."

" Your question is easily answered," said
the hall-porter.   " I would go around the
corner and get me a nice stiff drink at Mike's
Place."

" A drink ? "

" Yes, sir.   A nice stiff one."

" At—where did you say ? "

"Mike's Place, sir. Just round the corner. You can't miss it."

William thanked him and walked away. The man's words had started a new, and in many ways interesting, train of thought. A drink? And a nice stiff one? There might be something in it.

William Mulliner had never tasted alcohol in his life. He had promised his late mother that he would not do so until he was either twenty-one or forty-one—he could never remember which. He was at present twenty-nine; but wishing to be on the safe side in case he had got his figures wrong, he had remained a teetotaller. But now, as he walked listlessly along the street towards the corner, it seemed to him that his mother in the special circumstances could not reasonably object if he took a slight snort. He raised his eyes to heaven, as though to ask her if a couple of quick ones might not be permitted; and he fancied that a faint, far-off voice whispered, "Go to it!"

And at this moment he found himself standing outside a brightly-lighted saloon.

For an instant he hesitated. Then, as a twinge of anguish in the region of his broken

heart reminded him of the necessity for immediate remedies, he pushed open the swing
doors and went in.

The principal feature of the cheerful,
brightly-lit room in which he found himself
was a long counter, at which were standing
a number of the citizenry, each with an elbow
on the woodwork and a foot upon the neat
brass rail which ran below. Behind the
counter appeared the upper section of one of
the most benevolent and kindly-looking men
that William had ever seen. He had a
large smooth face, and he wore a white coat,
and he eyed William, as he advanced, with a
sort of reverent joy.

" Is this Mike's Place ? " asked William.

" Yes, sir," replied the white-coated man.

" Are you Mike ? "

" No, sir. But I am his representative,
and have full authority to act on his behalf.
What can I have the pleasure of doing for
you ? "

The man's whole attitude made him seem so
like a large-hearted elder brother that William
felt no diffidence about confiding in him. He
placed an elbow on the counter and a foot on
the rail, and spoke with a sob in his voice.

"Suppose the only girl you had ever loved had gone and got engaged to another, what in your view would best meet the case?"

The gentlemanly bar-tender pondered for some moments.

"Well," he replied at length, " I advance it, you understand, as a purely personal opinion, and I shall not be in the least offended if you decide not to act upon it ; but my suggestion—for what it is worth—is that you try a Dynamite Dew-Drop."

One of the crowd that had gathered sympathetically round shook his head. He was a charming man with a black eye, who had shaved on the preceding Thursday.

"Much better give him a Dreamland Special."

A second man, in a sweater and a cloth cap, had yet another theory.

"You can't beat an Undertaker's Joy."

They were all so perfectly delightful and appeared to have his interests so un-selfishly at heart that William could not bring himself to choose between them. He solved the problem in diplomatic fashion by playing no favourites and ordering all three of the beverages recommended.

The effect was instantaneous and grati-
fying. As he drained the first glass, it
seemed to him that a torchlight procession,
of whose existence he had hitherto not been
aware, had begun to march down his throat
and explore the recesses of his stomach.
The second glass, though slightly too heavily
charged with molten lava, was extremely
palatable. It helped the torchlight procession along by adding to it a brass band of
singular power and sweetness of tone. And
with the third somebody began to touch off
fireworks inside his head.

William felt better—not only spiritually
but physically. He seemed to himself to be
a bigger, finer man, and the loss of Myrtle
Banks had somehow in a flash lost nearly
all its importance. After all, as he said to
the man with the black eye, Myrtle Banks
wasn't everybody.

" Now what do you recommend ? " he
asked the man with the sweater, having
turned the last glass upside down.

The other mused, one fore-finger thoughtfully pressed against the side of his face.

" Well, I'll tell you," he said. " When
my brother Elmer lost his girl, he drank

straight rye. Yes, sir. That's what he drank—straight rye. ' I've lost my girl,' he said, ' and I'm going to drink straight rye.' That's what he said. Yes, sir, straight rye."

" And was your brother Elmer," asked William, anxiously, " a man whose example in your opinion should be followed? Was he a man you could trust ? "

" He owned the biggest duck-farm in the southern half of Illinois."

" That settles it," said William. " What was good enough for a duck who owned half Illinois is good enough for me. Oblige me," he said to the gentlemanly bar-tender, " by asking these gentlemen what they will have, and start pouring."

The bar-tender obeyed, and William, having tried a pint or two of the strange liquid just to see if he liked it, found that he did, and ordered some. He then began to move about among his new friends, patting one on the shoulder, slapping another affably on the back, and asking a third what his Christian name was.

" I want you all," he said, climbing on to the counter so that his voice should carry better, " to come and stay with me in England.   Never in my life have I met men whose faces I liked so much.   More like brothers than anything is the way I regard you.   So just you pack up a few things and come along and put up at my little place for as long as you can manage.   You particularly, my dear old chap," he added, beaming at the man in the sweater.

" Thanks," said the man with the sweater.

" What did you say ? " said William.

" I said, ' Thanks.' "

William slowly removed his coat and rolled up his shirt-sleeves.

" I call you gentlemen to witness," he said, quietly, " that I have been grossly insulted by this gentleman who has just grossly insulted me.   I am not a quarrelsome man, but if anybody wants a row they can have it.   And when it comes to being cursed and sworn at by an ugly bounder in a sweater and a cloth cap, it is time to take steps."

And with these spirited words William Mulliner sprang from the counter, grasped the other by the throat, and bit him sharply on the right ear.   There was a confused interval, during which somebody attached himself to the collar of William's waistcoat and the seat of William's trousers, and then a sense of swift movement and rush of cool air.

William discovered that he was seated on the pavement outside the saloon. A hand emerged from the swing door and threw his hat out. And he was alone with the night and his meditations.

These were, as you may suppose, of a singularly bitter nature. Sorrow and disillusionment racked William Mulliner like a physical pain. That his friends inside there, in spite of the fact that he had been all sweetness and light and had not done a thing to them, should have thrown him out into the hard street was the saddest thing he had ever heard of ; and for some minutes he sat there, weeping silently.

Presently he heaved himself to his feet and, placing one foot with infinite delicacy in front of the other, and then drawing the other one up and placing it with infinite delicacy in front of that, he began to walk back to his hotel.

At the corner he paused. There were some railings on his right. He clung to them and rested awhile.

The railings to which William Mulliner had attached himself belonged to a brown-stone house of the kind that seems destined from the first moment of its building to receive guests, both resident and transient, at a moderate weekly rental. It was, in fact, as he would have discovered had he been clear-sighted enough to read the card over the door, Mrs. Beulah O'Brien's Theatrical Boarding-House (" A Home From Home—No Cheques Cashed—This Means You ").

But William was not in the best of shape for reading cards. A sort of mist had obscured the world, and he was finding it difficult to keep his eyes open. And presently, his chin wedged into the railings, he fell into a dreamless sleep.

He was awakened by light flashing in his eyes ; and, opening them, saw that a window opposite where he was standing had become brightly illuminated. His slumbers had cleared his vision ; and he was able to observe that the room into which he was looking was a dining-room. The long table was set for the evening meal ; and to William, as he gazed, the sight of that cosy apartment, with

the gaslight falling on the knives and forks
and spoons, seemed the most pathetic and
poignant that he had ever beheld.

A mood of the most extreme sentimentality now had him in its grip. The thought
that he would never own a little home like
that racked him from stem to stern with an
almost unbearable torment. What, argued
William, clinging to the railings and crying
weakly, could compare, when you came
right down to it, with a little home ? A
man with a little home is all right, whereas
a man without a little home is just a bit of
flotsam on the ocean of life. If Myrtle
Banks had only consented to marry him,
he would have had a little home. But she
had refused to marry him, so he would never
have a little home. What Myrtle Banks
wanted, felt William, was a good swift clout
on the side of the head.

The thought pleased him. He was feeling
physically perfect again now, and seemed
to have shaken off completely the slight
indisposition from which he had been suffering. His legs had lost their tendency to act
independently of the rest of his body. His
head felt clearer, and he had a sense of

overwhelming strength. If ever, in short, there was a moment when he could administer that clout on the side of the head to Myrtle Banks as it should be administered, that moment was now.

He was on the point of moving off to find her and teach her what it meant to stop a man like himself from having a little home, when some one entered the room into which he was looking, and he paused to make further inspection.

The new arrival was a coloured maid-servant. She staggered to the head of the table beneath the weight of a large tureen containing, so William suspected, hash. A moment later a stout woman with bright golden hair came in and sat down opposite the tureen.

The instinct to watch other people eat is one of the most deeply implanted in the human bosom, and William lingered, intent. There was, he told himself, no need to hurry. He knew which was Myrtle's room in the hotel. It was just across the corridor from his own. He could pop in any time, during the night, and give her that clout. Meanwhile, he wanted to watch these people eat hash.

And then the door opened again, and there filed into the room a little procession. And William, clutching the railings, watched it with bulging eyes.

The procession was headed by an elderly man in a check suit with a carnation in his buttonhole. He was about three feet six in height, though the military jauntiness with which he carried himself made him seem fully three feet seven. He was followed by a younger man who wore spectacles and whose height was perhaps three feet four. And behind these two came, in single file, six others, scaling down by degrees until, bringing up the rear of the procession, there entered a rather stout man in tweeds and bedroom slippers who could not have measured more than two feet eight.

They took their places at the table. Hash was distributed to all. And the man in tweeds, having inspected his plate with obvious relish, removed his slippers and, picking up his knife and fork with his toes, fell to with a keen appetite.

William Mulliner uttered a soft moan, and tottered away.

It was a black moment for my Uncle

William. Only an instant before he had been congratulating himself on having shaken off the effects of his first indulgence in alcohol after an abstinence of twenty-nine years; but now he perceived that he was still intoxicated.

Intoxicated? The word did not express it by a mile. He was oiled, boiled, fried, plastered, whiffled, sozzled, and blotto. Only by the exercise of the most consummate caution and address could he hope to get back to his hotel and reach his bedroom without causing an open scandal.

Of course, if his walk that night had taken him a few yards farther down the street than the door of Mike's Place, he would have seen that there was a very simple explanation of the spectacle which he had just witnessed. A walk so extended would have brought him to the San Francisco Palace of Varieties, outside which large posters proclaimed the exclusive engagement for two weeks of

MURPHY'S MIDGETS.

BIGGER AND BETTER THAN EVER.

But of the existence of these posters he was not aware; and it is not too much to

G

say that the iron entered into William Mulliner's soul.

That his legs should have become temporarily unscrewed at the joints was a phenomenon which he had been able to bear with fortitude. That his head should be feeling as if a good many bees had decided to use it as a hive was unpleasant, but not unbearably so. But that his brain should have gone off its castors and be causing him to see visions was the end of all things.

William had always prided himself on the keenness of his mental powers. All through the long voyage on the ship, when Desmond Franklyn had related anecdotes illustrative of his prowess as a man of Action, William Mulliner had always consoled himself by feeling that in the matter of brain he could give Franklyn three bisques and a beating any time he chose to start. And now, it seemed, he had lost even this advantage over his rival. For Franklyn, dull-witted clod though he might be, was not such an absolute minus quantity that he would imagine he had seen a man of two feet eight cutting up hash with his toes. That hideous depth of mental decay had been reserved for William Mulliner.

Moodily he made his way back to his hotel. In a corner of the Palm Room he saw Myrtle Banks deep in conversation with Franklyn, but all desire to give her a clout on the side of the head had now left him. With his chin sunk on his breast, he entered the elevator and was carried up to his room.

Here as rapidly as his quivering fingers would permit, he undressed ; and, climbing into the bed as it came round for the second time, lay for a space with wide-open eyes. He had been too shaken to switch his light off, and the rays of the lamp shone on the handsome ceiling which undulated above him. He gave himself up to thought once more.

No doubt, he felt, thinking it over now, his mother had had some very urgent reason for withholding him from alcoholic drink. She must have known of some family secret, sedulously guarded from his infant ears— some dark tale of a fatal Mulliner taint. "William must never learn of this ! " she had probably said when they told her the old legend of how every Mulliner for centuries back had died a maniac, victim at last to the fatal fluid. And to-night, despite her gentle care, he had found out for himself.

He saw now that this derangement of his eyesight was only the first step in the gradual dissolution which was the Mulliner Curse. Soon his sense of hearing would go, then his sense of touch.

He sat up in bed. It seemed to him that, as he gazed at the ceiling, a considerable section of it had parted from the parent body and fallen with a crash to the floor.

William Mulliner stared dumbly. He knew, of course, that it was an illusion. But what a perfect illusion! If he had not had the special knowledge which he possessed, he would have stated without fear of contradiction that there was a gap six feet wide above him and a mass of dust and plaster on the carpet below.

And even as his eyes deceived him, so did his ears. He seemed to be conscious of a babel of screams and shouts. The corridor, he could have sworn, was full of flying feet. The world appeared to be all bangs and crashes and thuds. A cold fear gripped at William's heart. His sense of hearing was playing tricks with him already.

His whole being recoiled from making the final experiment, but he forced himself out of bed. He reached a finger towards the nearest heap of plaster and drew it back with a groan. Yes, it was as he feared, his sense of touch had gone wrong too. That heap of plaster, though purely a figment of his disordered brain, had felt solid.

So there it was. One little moderately festive evening at Mike's Place, and the Curse of the Mulliners had got him. Within an hour of absorbing the first drink of his life, it had deprived him of his sight, his hearing, and his sense of touch. Quick service, felt William Mulliner.

As he climbed back into bed, it appeared to him that two of the walls fell out. He shut his eyes, and presently sleep, which has been well called Tired Nature's Sweet Restorer, brought oblivion. His last waking thought was that he imagined he had heard another wall go.

William Mulliner was a sound sleeper, and it was many hours before consciousness returned to him. When he awoke, he looked about him in astonishment. The haunting horror of the night had passed ; and now, though conscious of a rather severe headache, he knew that he was seeing things as they were.

And yet it seemed odd to think that what he beheld was not the remains of some nightmare. Not only was the world slightly yellow and a bit blurred about the edges, but it had changed in its very essentials overnight. Where eight hours before there had been a wall, only an open space appeared, with bright sunlight streaming through it. The ceiling was on the floor, and almost the only thing remaining of what had been an expensive bedroom in a first-class hotel was the bed. Very strange, he thought, and very irregular.

A voice broke in upon his meditations.

" Why, Mr. Mulliner ! "

William turned, and being, like all the Mulliners, the soul of modesty, dived abruptly beneath the bed-clothes. For the voice was the voice of Myrtle Banks. And she was in his room !

" Mr. Mulliner ! "

William poked his head out cautiously. And then he perceived that the proprieties had not been outraged as he had imagined.

Miss Banks was not in his room, but in the corridor. The intervening wall had disappeared. Shaken, but relieved, he sat up in bed, the sheet drawn round his shoulders.

" You don't mean to say you're still in bed ? " gasped the girl.

" Why, is it awfully late ? " said William.

" Did you actually stay up here all through it ? "

" Through what ? "

" The earthquake."

" What earthquake ? "

" The earthquake last night."

" Oh, that earthquake ? " said William, carelessly. " I did notice some sort of an earthquake. I remember seeing the ceiling come down and saying to myself, ' I shouldn't wonder if that wasn't an earthquake.' And then the walls fell out, and I said, ' Yes, I believe it *is* an earthquake.' And then I turned over and went to sleep."

Myrtle Banks was staring at him with eyes that reminded him partly of twin stars and partly of a snail's.

" You must be the bravest man in the world ! "

William gave a curt laugh.

" Oh, well," he said, " I may not spend my whole life persecuting unfortunate sharks with pocket-knives, but I find I generally manage to keep my head fairly well in a crisis.   We Mulliners are like that.   We do not say much, but we have the right stuff in us."

He clutched his head.   A sharp spasm had reminded him how much of the right stuff he had in him at that moment.

" My hero ! " breathed the girl, almost inaudibly.

" And how is your fiancé this bright, sunny morning ? " asked William, nonchalantly.   It was torture to refer to the man, but he must show her that a Mulliner knew how to take his medicine.

She gave a little shudder.

" I have no fiancé," she said.

" But I thought you told me you and Franklyn . . ."

" I am no longer engaged to Mr. Franklyn. Last night, when the earthquake started, I cried to him to help me ; and he with a hasty ' Some other time ! ' over his shoulder, disappeared into the open like something shot out of a gun.   I never saw a man run so fast.

This morning I broke off the engagement."
She uttered a scornful laugh.

" Sharks and pocket-knives !   I don't believe he ever killed a shark in his life."

" And even if he did," said William,
" what of it ?   I mean to say, how in-
frequently in married life must the necessity
for killing sharks with pocket-knives arise !
What a husband needs is not some purely
adventitious gift like that—a parlour trick,
you might almost call it—but a steady
character, a warm and generous disposition,
and a loving heart."

" How true ! " she murmured, dreamily.

" Myrtle," said William, " I would be a
husband like that.   The steady character,
the warm and generous disposition, and
the loving heart to which I have alluded
are at your disposal.   Will you accept
them ? "

" I will," said Myrtle Banks.

And that (concluded Mr. Mulliner) is the
story of my Uncle William's romance.   And
you will readily understand, having heard
it, how his eldest son, my cousin, J. S. F. E.
Mulliner, got his name.

G 2

" J. S. F. E. ? " I said.

" John San Francisco Earthquake Mulliner," explained my friend.

" There never was a San Francisco earthquake," said the Californian. " Only a fire."

VII

PORTRAIT OF A DISCIPLINARIAN

I T was with something of the relief of fog-
bound city-dwellers who at last behold
the sun that we perceived, on entering
the bar-parlour of the Anglers' Rest, that
Mr. Mulliner was seated once more in the
familiar chair. For some days he had been
away, paying a visit to an old nurse of his
down in Devonshire : and there was no
doubt that in his absence the tide of
intellectual conversation had run very
low.

"No," said Mr. Mulliner, in answer to a
question as to whether he had enjoyed
himself, "I cannot pretend that it was an
altogether agreeable experience. I was conscious throughout of a sense of strain. The
poor old thing is almost completely deaf, and
her memory is not what it was. Moreover,

it is a moot point whether a man of sensibility can ever be entirely at his ease in the presence of a woman who has frequently spanked him with the flat side of a hairbrush."

Mr. Mulliner winced slightly, as if the old wound still troubled him.

"It is curious," he went on, after a thoughtful pause, "how little change the years bring about in the attitude of a real, genuine, crusted old family nurse towards one who in the early knickerbocker stage of his career has been a charge of hers. He may grow grey or bald and be looked up to by the rest of his world as a warm performer on the Stock Exchange or a devil of a fellow in the sphere of Politics or the Arts, but to his old Nanna he will still be the Master James or Master Percival who had to be hounded by threats to keep his face clean. Shakespeare would have cringed before his old nurse. So would Herbert Spencer, Attila the Hun, and the Emperor Nero. My nephew Frederick . . . but I must not bore you with my family gossip."

We reassured him.

"Oh well, if you wish to hear the story.

There is nothing much in it as a story, but it bears out the truth of what I have just been saying."

I will begin (said Mr. Mulliner) at the moment when Frederick, having come down from London in response to an urgent summons from his brother, Doctor George Mulliner, stood in the latter's consulting-room, looking out upon the Esplanade of that quiet little watering-place, Bingley-on-Sea.

George's consulting-room, facing west, had the advantage of getting the afternoon sun : and this afternoon it needed all the sun it could get, to counteract Frederick's extraordinary gloom. The young man's expression, as he confronted his brother, was that which a miasmic pool in some dismal swamp in the Bad Lands might have worn if it had had a face.

" Then the position, as I see it," he said in a low, toneless voice, " is this. On the pretext of wishing to discuss urgent family business with me, you have dragged me down to this foul spot—seventy miles by rail in a compartment containing three distinct infants sucking sweets—merely to have tea with a nurse whom I have disliked since I was a child."

"You have contributed to her support for many years," George reminded him.

"Naturally, when the family were clubbing together to pension off the old blister, I chipped in with my little bit," said Frederick. "Noblesse oblige."

"Well, noblesse obliges you to go and have tea with her when she invites you. Wilks must be humoured. She is not so young as she was."

"She must be a hundred."

"Eighty-five."

"Good heavens! And it seems only yesterday that she shut me up in a cupboard for stealing jam."

"She was a great disciplinarian," agreed George. "You may find her a little on the autocratic side still. And I want to impress upon you, as her medical man, that you must not thwart her lightest whim. She will probably offer you boiled eggs and home-made cake. Eat them."

"I will not eat boiled eggs at five o'clock in the afternoon," said Frederick, with a strong man's menacing calm, " for any woman on earth."

" You will. And with relish. Her heart is weak. If you don't humour her, I won't answer for the consequences."

" If I eat boiled eggs at five in the afternoon, I won't answer for the consequences. And why boiled eggs, dash it ? I'm not a schoolboy."

" To her you are. She looks on all of us as children still. Last Christmas she gave me a copy of *Eric, or Little by Little.*"

Frederick turned to the window, and scowled down upon the noxious and depressing scene below. Sparing neither age nor sex in his detestation, he regarded the old ladies reading their library novels on the seats with precisely the same dislike and contempt which he bestowed on the boys' school clattering past on its way to the bathing-houses.

" Then, checking up your statements," he said, " I find that I am expected to go to tea with a woman who, in addition, apparently, to being a blend of Lucretia Borgia and a Prussian sergeant-major, is a physical wreck and practically potty. Why ? That is what I ask. Why ? As a child, I objected strongly to Nurse Wilks : and now, grown to riper years, the thought of meeting her again gives me the heeby-jeebies. Why should I be victimised ? Why me particularly ? "

" It isn't you particularly. We've all been to see her at intervals, and so have the Oliphants."

" The Oliphants ! "

The name seemed to affect Frederick oddly. He winced, as if his brother had been a dentist instead of a general practitioner and had just drawn one of his back teeth.

" She was their nurse after she left us. You can't have forgotten the Oliphants. I remember you at the age of twelve climbing that old elm at the bottom of the paddock to get Jane Oliphant a rook's egg."

Frederick laughed bitterly.

" I must have been a perfect ass. Fancy risking my life for a girl like that ! Not," he went on, " that life's worth much. An absolute wash-out, that's what life is. However, it will soon be over. And then the silence and peace of the grave. That," said Frederick, " is the thought that sustains me."

" A pretty kid, Jane. Some one told me she had grown up quite a beauty."

" Without a heart."

" What do you know about it ? "

" Merely this. She pretended to love me, and then a few months ago she went off to the country to stay with some people named Ponderby and wrote me a letter breaking off the engagement. She gave no reasons, and I have not seen her since. She is now engaged to a man named Dillingwater, and I hope it chokes her."

" I never heard about this. I'm sorry."

" I'm not. Merciful release is the way I look at it."

" Would he be one of the Sussex Dilling-waters ? "

" I don't know what county the family infests. If I did, I would avoid it."

" Well, I'm sorry. No wonder you're depressed."

" Depressed ? " said Frederick, outraged. " Me ? You don't suppose I'm worrying myself about a girl like that, do you ? I've never been so happy in my life. I'm just bubbling over with cheerfulness."

" Oh, is that what it is ? " George looked

at his watch. " Well, you'd better be pushing along. It'll take you about ten minutes
to get to Marazion Road."

" How do I find the blasted house ? "

" The name's on the door."

" What is the name ? "

" Wee Holme."

" My God ! " said Frederick Mulliner.
" It only needed that ! "

The view which he had had of it from his
brother's window should, no doubt, have
prepared Frederick for the hideous loath-
someness of Bingley-on-Sea : but, as he
walked along, he found it coming on him as a
complete surprise. Until now he had never
imagined that a small town could possess
so many soul-searing features. He passed
little boys, and thought how repulsive little
boys were. He met tradesmen's carts, and
his gorge rose at the sight of them. He
hated the houses. And, most of all, he
objected to the sun. It shone down with
a cheeriness which was not only offensive
but, it seemed to Frederick Mulliner, deliberately offensive. What he wanted was wailing winds and driving rain : not a beastly
expanse of vivid blue. It was not that the

perfidy of Jane Oliphant had affected him in any way : it was simply that he disliked blue skies and sunshine. He had a temperamental antipathy for them, just as he had a temperamental fondness for tombs and sleet and hurricanes and earthquakes and famines and pestilences and . . .

He found that he had arrived in Marazion Road.

Marazion Road was made up of two spotless pavements stretching into the middle distance and flanked by two rows of neat little red-brick villas. It smote Frederick like a blow. He felt as he looked at those houses, with their little brass knockers and little white curtains, that they were occupied by people who knew nothing of Frederick Mulliner and were content to know nothing ; people who were simply not caring a whoop that only a few short months before the girl to whom he had been engaged had sent back his letters and gone and madly got herself betrothed to a man named Dillingwater.

He found Wee Holme, and hit it a nasty slap with its knocker. Footsteps sounded in the passage, and the door opened.

" Why, Master Frederick ! " said Nurse Wilks.   " I should hardly have known you."

Frederick, in spite of the natural gloom caused by the blue sky and the warm sunshine, found his mood lightening somewhat. Something that might almost have been a spasm of tenderness passed through him. He was not a bad-hearted young man—he ranked in that respect, he supposed, somewhere mid-way between his brother George, who had a heart of gold, and people like the future Mrs. Dillingwater, who had no heart at all—and there was a fragility about Nurse Wilks that first astonished and then touched him.

The images which we form in childhood are slow to fade : and Frederick had been under the impression that Nurse Wilks was fully six feet tall, with the shoulders of a weight-lifter and eyes that glittered cruelly beneath beetling brows.   What he saw now was a little old woman with a wrinkled face, who looked as if a puff of wind would blow her away.

He was oddly stirred.   He felt large and protective.   He saw his brother's point now.   Most certainly this frail old thing must be humoured. Only a brute would refuse to humour her—yes, felt Frederick Mulliner, even if it meant boiled eggs at five o'clock in the afternoon.

" Well, you are getting a big boy ! " said Nurse Wilks, beaming.

" Do you think so ? " said Frederick, with equal amiability.

" Quite the little man ! And all dressed up. Go into the parlour, dear, and sit down. I'm getting the tea."

" Thanks."

" WIPE YOUR BOOTS ! "

The voice, thundering from a quarter whence hitherto only soft cooings had proceeded, affected Frederick Mulliner a little like the touching off of a mine beneath his feet. Spinning round he perceived a different person altogether from the mild and kindly hostess of a moment back. It was plain that there yet lingered in Nurse Wilks not a little of the ancient fire. Her mouth was tightly compressed and her eyes gleamed dangerously.

" Theideaofyourbringingyournastydirty-bootsintomynicecleanhousewithoutwiping-them ! " said Nurse Wilks.

" Sorry ! " said Frederick humbly.

He burnished the criticised shoes on the mat, and tottered to the parlour. He felt much smaller, much younger and much feebler than he had felt a minute ago. His morale had been shattered into fragments.

And it was not pieced together by the sight, as he entered the parlour, of Miss Jane Oliphant sitting in an armchair by the window.

It is hardly to be supposed that the reader will be interested in the appearance of a girl of the stamp of Jane Oliphant—a girl capable of wantonly returning a good man's letters and going off and getting engaged to a Dillingwater : but one may as well describe her and get it over. She had golden-brown hair ; golden-brown eyes ; golden-brown eyebrows ; a nice nose with one freckle on the tip ; a mouth which, when it parted in a smile, disclosed pretty teeth ; and a resolute little chin.

At the present moment, the mouth was not parted in a smile. It was closed up tight, and the chin was more than resolute. It looked like the ram of a very small battleship. She gazed at Frederick as if he were the smell of onions, and she did not say a word.

Nor did Frederick say very much. Nothing is more difficult for a young man than to find exactly the right remark with which to open conversation with a girl who has recently returned his letters. (Darned good letters, too. Reading them over after opening the package, he had been amazed at their charm and eloquence.)

Frederick, then, confined his observations to the single word "Guk!" Having uttered this, he sank into a chair and stared at the carpet. The girl stared out of window : and complete silence reigned in the room till from the interior of a clock which was ticking on the mantelpiece a small wooden bird suddenly emerged, said "Cuckoo," and withdrew.

The abruptness of this bird's appearance and the oddly staccato nature of its diction could not but have their effect on a man whose nerves were not what they had been. Frederick Mulliner, rising some eighteen inches from his chair, uttered a hasty exclamation.

"I beg your pardon ? " said Jane Oliphant, raising her eyebrows.

" Well, how was I to know it was going to do that ? " said Frederick defensively.

Jane Oliphant shrugged her shoulders. The gesture seemed to imply supreme indifference to what the sweepings of the Underworld knew or did not know.

But Frederick, the ice being now in a manner broken, refused to return to the silence.

" What are you doing here ? " he said.

" I have come to have tea with Nanna."

" I didn't know you were going to be here."

" Oh ? "

" If I'd known that you were going to be here . . ."

" You've got a large smut on your nose."

Frederick gritted his teeth and reached for his handkerchief.

" Perhaps I'd better go," he said.

" You will do nothing of the kind," said Miss Oliphant sharply. " She is looking forward to seeing you. Though why . . ."

" Why ? " prompted Frederick coldly.

" Oh, nothing."

In the unpleasant silence which followed, broken only by the deep breathing of a man who was trying to choose the rudest out of the

three retorts which had presented themselves
to him, Nurse Wilks entered.

"It's just a suggestion," said Miss Oliphant aloofly, "but don't you think you
might help Nanna with that heavy tray?"

Frederick, roused from his preoccupation,
sprang to his feet, blushing the blush of
shame.

"You might have strained yourself,
Nanna," the girl went on, in a voice dripping
with indignant sympathy.

"I was going to help her," mumbled
Frederick.

"Yes, after she had put the tray down on
the table. Poor Nanna! How very heavy
it must have been."

Not for the first time since their acquaintance had begun, Frederick felt a sort of wistful
wonder at his erstwhile fiancée's uncanny
ability to put him in the wrong. His
emotions now were rather what they
would have been if he had been detected
striking his hostess with some blunt instrument.

"He always was a thoughtless boy," said
Nurse Wilks tolerantly. "Do sit down,
Master Frederick, and have your tea. I've

boiled some eggs for you. I know what a boy you always are for eggs."

Frederick, starting, directed a swift glance at the tray. Yes, his worst fears had been realised. Eggs—and large ones. A stomach which he had fallen rather into the habit of pampering of late years gave a little whimper of apprehension.

" Yes," proceeded Nurse Wilks, pursuing the subject, " you never could have enough eggs. Nor cake. Dear me, how sick you made yourself with cake that day at Miss Jane's birthday party."

" Please ! " said Miss Oliphant, with a slight shiver.

She looked coldly at her fermenting fellow-guest, as he sat plumbing the deepest abysses of self-loathing.

" No eggs for me, thank you," he said.

" Master Frederick, you will eat your nice boiled eggs," said Nurse Wilks. Her voice was still amiable, but there was a hint of dynamite behind it.

" I don't want any eggs."

" Master Frederick ! " The dynamite exploded. Once again that amazing transformation had taken place, and a frail little old woman had become an intimidating force with which only a Napoleon could have reckoned. "I will not have this sulking."

Frederick gulped.

"I'm sorry," he said, meekly. "I should enjoy an egg."

"Two eggs," corrected Nurse Wilks.

"Two eggs," said Frederick.

Miss Oliphant twisted the knife in the wound.

"There seems to be plenty of cake, too. How nice for you! Still, I should be careful, if I were you. It looks rather rich. I never could understand," she went on, addressing Nurse Wilks in a voice which Frederick, who was now about seven years old, considered insufferably grown-up and affected, "why people should find any enjoyment in stuffing and gorging and making pigs of themselves."

"Boys will be boys," argued Nurse Wilks.

"I suppose so," sighed Miss Oliphant. "Still, it's all rather unpleasant."

A slight but well-defined glitter appeared in Nurse Wilks' eyes. She detected a tendency to hoighty-toightiness in her young guest's manner, and hoighty-toightiness was a thing to be checked.

"Girls," she said, "are by no means perfect."

"Ah!" breathed Frederick, in rapturous adhesion to the sentiment.

"Girls have their little faults. Girls are sometimes inclined to be vain. I know a little girl not a hundred miles from this room who was so proud of her new panties that she ran out in the street in them."

"Nanna!" cried Miss Oliphant pinkly.

"Disgusting!" said Frederick.

He uttered a short laugh : and so full was this laugh, though short, of scorn, disdain, and a certain hideous masculine superiority, that Jane Oliphant's proud spirit writhed beneath the infliction. She turned on him with blazing eyes.

"What did you say?"

"I said 'Disgusting!'"

"Indeed?"

"I cannot," said Frederick judicially, "imagine a more deplorable exhibition, and I hope you were sent to bed without any supper."

"If you ever had to go without your supper," said Miss Oliphant, who believed in attack as the best form of defence, " it would kill you."

" Is that so ? " said Frederick.

" You're a beast, and I hate you," said Miss Oliphant.

" Is that so ? "

" Yes, that is so."

" Now, now, now," said Nurse Wilks. " Come, come, come ! "

She eyed the two with that comfortable look of power and capability which comes naturally to women who have spent half a century in dealing with the young and fractious.

" We will have no quarrelling," she said. " Make it up at once. Master Frederick, give Miss Jane a nice kiss."

The room rocked before Frederick's bulging eyes.

" A what ? " he gasped.

" Give her a nice big kiss and tell her you're sorry you quarrelled with her."

" She quarrelled with me."

" Never mind. A little gentleman must always take the blame."

Frederick, working desperately, dragged to the surface a sketchy smile.

" I apologise," he said.

" Don't mention it," said Miss Oliphant.

" Kiss her," said Nurse Wilks.

" I won't ! " said Frederick.

" What ! "

" I won't."

" Master Frederick," said Nurse Wilks, rising and pointing a menacing finger, " you march straight into that cupboard in the passage and stay there till you are good."

Frederick hesitated. He came of a proud family. A Mulliner had once received the thanks of his Sovereign for services rendered on the field of Crecy. But the recollection of what his brother George had said decided him. Infra dig. as it might be to allow himself to be shoved away in cupboards, it was better than being responsible for a woman's heart-failure. With bowed head he passed through the door, and a key clicked behind him.

All alone in a dark world that smelt of mice, Frederick Mulliner gave himself up to gloomy reflection. He had just put in about two minutes' intense thought of a kind which would have made the meditations of Schopenhauer on one of his bad mornings seem

like the day-dreams of Polyanna, when a
voice spoke through the crack in the door.

"Freddie. I mean Mr. Mulliner."

"Well?"

"She's gone into the kitchen to get the
jam," proceeded the voice rapidly. "Shall
I let you out?"

"Pray do not trouble," said Frederick
coldly. "I am perfectly comfortable."

Silence followed. Frederick returned to
his reverie. About now, he thought, but for
his brother George's treachery in luring him
down to this plague-spot by a misleading
telegram, he would have been on the twelfth
green at Squashy Hollow, trying out that
new putter. Instead of which . . .

The door opened abruptly, and as abruptly
closed again. And Frederick Mulliner, who
had been looking forward to an unbroken
solitude, discovered with a good deal of
astonishment that he had started taking in
lodgers.

"What are you doing here?" he
demanded, with a touch of proprietorial
disapproval.

The girl did not answer. But presently
muffled sounds came to him through the

darkness. In spite of himself, a certain tenderness crept upon Frederick.

" I say," he said awkwardly. " There's nothing to cry about."

" I'm not crying. I'm laughing."

" Oh ? " The tenderness waned. " You think it's amusing, do you, being shut up in this damned cupboard . . ."

" There is no need to use bad language."

` " I entirely disagree with you. There is every need to use bad language. It's ghastly enough being at Bingley-on-Sea at all, but when it comes to being shut up in Bingley cupboards . . ."

" . . . with a girl you hate ? "

" We will not go into that aspect of the matter," said Frederick with dignity. " The important point is that here I am in a cupboard at Bingley-on-Sea when, if there were any justice or right-thinking in the world, I should be out at Squashy Hollow . . ."

" Oh ? Do you still play golf ? "

" Certainly I still play golf. Why not ? "

" I don't know why not. I'm glad you are still able to amuse yourself."

" How do you mean, still ? Do you think that just because . . . ? "

" I don't think anything."

" I suppose you imagined I would be creeping about the place, a broken-hearted wreck ? "

" Oh no. I knew you would find it very easy to console yourself."

" What do you mean by that ? "

" Never mind."

" Are you insinuating that I am the sort of man who turns lightly from one woman to another—a mere butterfly who flits from flower to flower, sipping . . . ? "

" Yes, if you want to know, I think you are a born sipper."

Frederick started. The charge was monstrous.

" I have never sipped. And, what's more, I have never flitted."

" That's funny."

" What's funny ? "

" What you said."

" You appear to have a very keen sense of humour," said Frederick weightily. " It amuses you to be shut up in cupboards. It amuses you to hear me say . . ."

" Well, it's nice to be able to get some amusement out of life, isn't it ? Do you

H

want to know why she shut me up in here ? "

" I haven't the slightest curiosity. Why ? "

" I forgot where I was and lighted a cigarette. Oh, my goodness ! "

" Now what ? "

" I thought I heard a mouse. Do you think there are mice in this cupboard ? "

" Certainly," said Frederick. " Dozens of them."

He would have gone on to specify the kind of mice,—large, fat, slithery, active mice : but at this juncture something hard and sharp took him agonisingly on the ankle.

" Ouch ! " cried Frederick.

" Oh, I'm sorry. Was that you ? "

" It was."

" I was kicking about to discourage the mice."

" I see."

" Did it hurt much ? "

" Only a trifle more than blazes, thank you for inquiring."

" I'm sorry."

" So am I."

" Anyway, it would have given a mouse a nasty jar, if it had been one, wouldn't it ? "

" The shock, I should imagine, of a life-time."

" Well, I'm sorry."

" Don't mention it. Why should I worry about a broken ankle, when . . ."

" When what ? "

" I forget what I was going to say."

" When your heart is broken ? "

" My heart is not broken." It was a point which Frederick wished to make lumin-ously clear. " I am gay . . . happy . . . Who the devil is this man Dillingwater ? " he concluded abruptly.

There was a momentary pause.

" Oh, just a man."

" Where did you meet him ? "

" At the Ponderbys'."

" Where did you get engaged to him ? "

" At the Ponderbys'."

" Did you pay another visit to the Ponderbys, then ? "

" No."

Frederick choked.

" When you went to stay with the Ponderbys, you were engaged to me. Do

you mean to say you broke off your engagement to me, met this Dillingwater, and got
engaged to him all in the course of a single
visit lasting barely two weeks ? "

" Yes."

Frederick said nothing. It struck him
later that he should have said " Oh, Woman,
Woman ! " but at the moment it did not
occur to him.

" I don't see what right you have to
criticise me," said Jane.

" Who criticised you ? "

" You did."

" When ? "

" Just then."

" I call Heaven to witness," cried
Frederick Mulliner, " that not by so much as
a single word have I hinted at my opinion
that your conduct is the vilest and most
revolting that has ever been drawn to my
attention. I never so much as suggested
that your revelation had shocked me to the
depths of my soul."

" Yes, you did. You sniffed."

" If Bingley-on-Sea is not open for being
sniffed in at this season," said Frederick
coldly, " I should have been informed earlier."

" I had a perfect right to get engaged to any one I liked and as quick as I liked, after the abominable way you behaved."

" Abominable way I behaved ? What do you mean ? "

" You know."

" Pardon me, I do not know. If you are alluding to my refusal to wear the tie you bought for me on my last birthday, I can but repeat my statement, made to you at the time, that, apart from being the sort of tie no upright man would be seen dead in a ditch with, its colours were those of a Cycling, Angling, and Dart-Throwing club of which I am not a member."

" I am not alluding to that. I mean the day I was going to the Ponderbys' and you promised to see me off at Paddington, and then you 'phoned and said you couldn't as you were detained by important business, and I thought, well, I think I'll go by the later train after all because that will give me time to lunch quietly at the Berkeley, and I went and lunched quietly at the Berkeley, and when I was there who should I see but you at a table at the other end of the room gorging yourself in the company of a beastly creature in a pink frock and henna'd hair. That's what I mean."

Frederick clutched at his forehead.

" Repeat that," he exclaimed.

Jane did so.

" Ye gods ! " said Frederick.

" It was like a blow over the head. Something seemed to snap inside me, and . . ."

" I can explain all," said Frederick.

Jane's voice in the darkness was cold.

" Explain ? " she said.

" Explain," said Frederick.

" All ? "

" All."

Jane coughed.

" Before beginning," she said, " do not forget that I know every one of your female relatives by sight."

" I don't want to talk about my female relatives."

" I thought you were going to say that she was one of them—an aunt or something."

" Nothing of the kind. She was a revue star. You probably saw her in a piece called ' Toot-Toot.' "

" And that is your idea of an explanation ! "

Frederick raised his hand for silence. Realising that she could not see it, he lowered it again.

"Jane," he said in a low, throbbing voice, "can you cast your mind back to a morning in the spring when we walked, you and I, in Kensington Gardens? The sun shone brightly, the sky was a limpid blue flecked with fleecy clouds, and from the west there blew a gentle breeze . . ."

"If you think you can melt me with that sort of . . ."

"Nothing of the kind. What I was leading up to was this. As we walked, you and I, there came snuffling up to us a small Pekingese dog. It left me, I admit, quite cold, but you went into ecstasies : and from that moment I had but one mission in life, to discover who that Peke belonged to and buy it for you. And after the most exhaustive inquiries, I tracked the animal down. It was the property of the lady in whose company you saw me lunching— lightly, not gorging—at the Berkeley that day. I managed to get an introduction to her, and immediately began to make offers to her for the dog. Money was no object to

me. All I wished was to put the little beast
in your arms and see your face light up. It
was to be a surprise. That morning the
woman 'phoned, and said that she had
practically decided to close with my latest
bid, and would I take her to lunch and discuss
the matter ? It was agony to have to ring
you up and tell you that I could not see you
off at Paddington, but it had to be done.
It was anguish having to sit for two hours
listening to that highly-coloured female telling
me how the comedian had ruined her big
number in her last show by standing up-
stage and pretending to drink ink, but that
had to be done too. I bit the bullet and
saw it through and I got the dog that afternoon. And next morning I received your
letter breaking off the engagement."

There was a long silence.

" Is this true ? " said Jane.

" Quite true."

" It sounds too—how shall I put it ?—
too frightfully probable. Look me in the
face ! "

" What's the good of looking you in the
face when I can't see an inch in front of me ? "

" Well, is it true ? "

" Certainly it is true."

" Can you produce the Peke ? "

" I have not got it on my person," said Frederick stiffly. " But it is at my flat, probably chewing up a valuable rug. I will give it you for a wedding present."

" Oh, Freddie ! "

" A wedding present," repeated Frederick, though the words stuck in his throat like patent American health-cereal.

" But I'm not going to be married."

" You're—what did you say ? "

" I'm not going to be married."

" But what of Dillingwater ? "

" That's off."

" Off ? "

" Off," said Jane firmly. " I only got engaged to him out of pique. I thought I could go through with it, buoying myself up by thinking what a score it would be off you, but one morning I saw him eating a peach and I began to waver. He splashed himself to the eyebrows. And just after that I found that he had a trick of making a sort of funny noise when he drank coffee. I would sit on the other side of the breakfast table, looking at him and saying to myself ' Now comes the funny noise ! ' and when I thought of doing that all the rest of my life I saw that the scheme was impossible. So I broke off the engagement."

Frederick gasped.

" Jane ! "

He groped out, found her, and drew her into his arms.

" Freddie ! "

" Jane ! "

" Freddie ! "

" Jane ! "

" Freddie ! "

" Jane ! "

On the panel of the door there sounded an authoritative rap. Through it there spoke an authoritative voice, slightly cracked by age but full, nevertheless, of the spirit that will stand no nonsense.

" Master Frederick."

" Hullo ? "

" Are you good now ? "

" You bet I'm good."

" Will you give Miss Jane a nice kiss ? "

" I will do," said Frederick Mulliner, enthusiasm ringing in every syllable, " just that little thing ! "

"Then you may come out," said Nurse Wilks. "I have boiled you two more eggs."

Frederick paled, but only for an instant. What did anything matter now? His lips were set in a firm line, and his voice, when he spoke, was calm and steady.

"Lead me to them," he said.

VIII

THE ROMANCE OF A BULB-SQUEEZER

SOMEBODY had left a copy of an illustrated weekly paper in the bar-parlour of the Anglers' Rest; and, glancing through it, I came upon the ninth full-page photograph of a celebrated musical comedy actress that I had seen since the preceding Wednesday. This one showed her looking archly over her shoulder with a rose between her teeth, and I flung the periodical from me with a stifled cry.

"Tut, tut!" said Mr. Mulliner, reprovingly. "You must not allow these things to affect you so deeply. Remember, it is not actresses' photographs that matter, but the courage which we bring to them."

He sipped his hot Scotch.

I wonder if you have ever reflected

(he said gravely) what life must be like for
the men whose trade it is to make these
pictures ? Statistics show that the two
classes of the community which least often
marry are milkmen and fashionable photographers—milkmen because they see women
too early in the morning, and fashionable
photographers because their days are spent
in an atmosphere of feminine loveliness so
monotonous that they become surfeited and
morose. I know of none of the world's
workers whom I pity more sincerely than the
fashionable photographer ; and yet—by one
of those strokes of irony which make the
thoughtful man waver between sardonic
laughter and sympathetic tears—it is the
ambition of every youngster who enters the
profession some day to become one.

At the outset of his career, you see, a
young photographer is sorely oppressed by
human gargoyles : and gradually this begins
to prey upon his nerves.

"Why is it," I remember my cousin
Clarence saying, after he had been about
a year in the business, "that all these misfits
want to be photographed ? Why do men
with faces which you would have thought

they would be anxious to hush up wish
to be strewn about the country on what-
nots and in albums ?   I started out full of
ardour and enthusiasm, and my eager soul
is being crushed.   This morning the Mayor
of Tooting East came to make an appointment.   He is coming to-morrow afternoon
to be taken in his cocked hat and robes of
office ;   and there is absolutely no excuse
for a man with a face like that perpetuating
his features.   I wish to goodness I was one
of those fellows who only take camera-
portraits of beautiful women."

His dream was to come true sooner than
he had imagined.   Within a week the great
test-case of Biggs v. Mulliner had raised my
cousin Clarence from an obscure studio in
West Kensington to the position of London's
most famous photographer.

You possibly remember the case ?   The
events that led up to it were, briefly, as
follows :—

Jno. Horatio Biggs, O.B.E., the newly-
elected Mayor of Tooting East, alighted from
a cab at the door of Clarence Mulliner's
studio at four-ten on the afternoon of June
the seventeenth.   At four-eleven he went in.

And at four-sixteen and a half he was observed shooting out of a first-floor window, vigorously assisted by my cousin, who was prodding him in the seat of the trousers with the sharp end of a photographic tripod. Those who were in a position to see stated that Clarence's face was distorted by a fury scarcely human.

Naturally the matter could not be expected to rest there. A week later the case of Biggs *v.* Mulliner had begun, the plaintiff claiming damages to the extent of ten thousand pounds and a new pair of trousers. And at first things looked very black for Clarence.

It was the speech of Sir Joseph Bodger, K.C., briefed for the defence, that turned the scale.

" I do not," said Sir Joseph, addressing the jury on the second day, " propose to deny the charges which have been brought against my client. We freely admit that on the seventeenth inst. we did jab the defendant with our tripod in a manner calculated to cause alarm and despondency. But, gentlemen, we plead justification. The whole case turns upon one question. Is a photographer

entitled to assault—either with or, as the
case may be, without a tripod—a sitter who,
after being warned that his face is not up to
the minimum standard requirements, insists
upon remaining in the chair and moistening
the lips with the tip of the tongue ?   Gentlemen, I say Yes !

" Unless you decide in favour of my
client, gentlemen of the jury, photographers
—debarred by law from the privilege of
rejecting sitters—will be at the mercy of
anyone who comes along with the price of a
dozen photographs in his pocket.   You have
seen the plaintiff, Biggs.   You have noted
his broad, slab-like face, intolerable to any
man of refinement and sensibility.   You
have observed his walrus moustache, his
double chin, his protruding eyes.   Take
another look at him, and then tell me if my
client was not justified in chasing him with a
tripod out of that sacred temple of Art and
Beauty, his studio.

" Gentlemen, I have finished.   I leave
my client's fate in your hands with every
confidence that you will return the only
verdict that can conceivably issue from
twelve men of your obvious intelligence,

your manifest sympathy, and your superb breadth of vision."

Of course, after that there was nothing to it. The jury decided in Clarence's favour without leaving the box ; and the crowd waiting outside to hear the verdict carried him shoulder-high to his house, refusing to disperse until he had made a speech and sung Photographers never, never, never shall be slaves. And next morning every paper in England came out with a leading article commending him for having so courageously established, as it had not been established since the days of Magna Charta, the fundamental principle of the Liberty of the Subject.

The effect of this publicity on Clarence's fortunes was naturally stupendous. He had become in a flash the best-known photographer in the United Kingdom, and was now in a position to realise that vision which he had of taking the pictures of none but the beaming and the beautiful. Every day the loveliest ornaments of Society and the Stage flocked to his studio ; and it was with the utmost astonishment, therefore, that, calling upon him one morning on my return to England after an absence of two years in the East, I learned that Fame and Wealth had not brought him happiness.

I found him sitting moodily in his studio, staring with dull eyes at a camera-portrait of a well-known actress in a bathing-suit. He looked up listlessly as I entered.

" Clarence ! " I cried, shocked at his appearance, for there were hard lines about his mouth and wrinkles on a forehead that once had been smooth as alabaster. " What is wrong ? "

" Everything," he replied, " I'm fed up."

" What with ? "

" Life. Beautiful women. This beastly photography business."

I was amazed. Even in the East rumours of his success had reached me, and on my return to London I found that they had not been exaggerated. In every photographers' club in the Metropolis, from the Negative and Solution in Pall Mall to the humble public-houses frequented by the men who do your pictures while you wait on the sands at seaside resorts, he was being freely spoken of as the logical successor to the

Presidency of the Amalgamated Guild of Bulb-Squeezers.

" I can't stick it much longer," said Clarence, tearing the camera-portrait into a dozen pieces with a dry sob and burying his face in his hands. " Actresses nursing their dolls ! Countesses simpering over kittens ! Film stars among their books ! In ten minutes I go to catch a train at Waterloo. I have been sent for by the Duchess of Hampshire to take some studies of Lady Monica Southbourne in the castle grounds."

A shudder ran through him. I patted him on the shoulder. I understood now.

" She has the most brilliant smile in England," he whispered.

" Come, come ! "

" Coy yet roguish, they tell me."

" It may not be true."

" And I bet she will want to be taken offering a lump of sugar to her dog, and the picture will appear in *The Sketch* and *Tatler* as ' Lady Monica Southbourne and Friend.' "

" Clarence, this is morbid."

He was silent for a moment.

" Ah, well," he said, pulling himself

together with a visible effort, " I have made my sodium sulphite, and I must lie in it."

I saw him off in a cab. The last view I had of him was of his pale, drawn profile. He looked, I thought, like an aristocrat of the French Revolution being borne off to his doom on a tumbril. How little he guessed that the only girl in the world lay waiting for him round the corner.

No, you are wrong. Lady Monica did not turn out to be the only girl in the world. If what I said caused you to expect that, I misled you. Lady Monica proved to be all his fancy had pictured her. In fact even more. Not only was her smile coy yet roguish, but she had a sort of coquettish droop of the left eyelid of which no one had warned him. And, in addition to her two dogs, which she was portrayed in the act of feeding with two lumps of sugar, she possessed a totally unforeseen pet monkey, of which he was compelled to take no fewer than eleven studies.

No, it was not Lady Monica who captured Clarence's heart, but a girl in a taxi whom he met on his way to the station.

It was in a traffic jam at the top of White-
hall that he first observed this girl. His cab
had become becalmed in a sea of omnibuses,
and, chancing to look to the right, he perceived within a few feet of him another taxi,
which had been heading for Trafalgar Square.
There was a face at its window. It turned
towards him, and their eyes met.

To most men it would have seemed an
unattractive face. To Clarence, surfeited
with the coy, the beaming, and the delicately-
chiselled, it was the most wonderful thing he
had ever looked at. All his life, he felt, he
had been searching for something on these
lines. That snub nose—those freckles—that
breadth of cheek-bone—the squareness of
that chin. And not a dimple in sight. He
told me afterwards that his only feeling at
first was one of incredulity. He had not
believed that the world contained women
like this. And then the traffic jam loosened
up and he was carried away.

It was as he was passing the Houses of
Parliament that the realisation came to him
that the strange bubbly sensation that seemed
to start from just above the lower left side-
pocket of his waistcoat was not, as he had

at first supposed, dyspepsia, but love. Yes, love had come at long last to Clarence Mulliner ; and for all the good it was likely to do him, he reflected bitterly, it might just as well have been the dyspepsia for which he had mistaken it. He loved a girl whom he would probably never see again. He did not know her name or where she lived or anything about her. All he knew was that he would cherish her image in his heart for ever, and that the thought of going on with the old dreary round of photographing lovely women with coy yet roguish smiles was almost more than he could bear.

However, custom is strong ; and a man who has once allowed the bulb-squeezing habit to get a grip of him cannot cast it off in a moment. Next day Clarence was back in his studio, diving into the velvet nose-bag as of yore and telling peeresses to watch the little birdie just as if nothing had happened. And if there was now a strange, haunting look of pain in his eyes, nobody objected to that. Indeed, inasmuch as the grief which gnawed at his heart had the effect of deepening and mellowing his camera-side manner to an almost sacerdotal unctuousness, his private sorrows actually helped his professional prestige. Women told one another that being photographed by Clarence Mulliner was like undergoing some wonderful spiritual experience in a noble cathedral ; and his appointment-book became fuller than ever.

So great now was his reputation that to anyone who had had the privilege of being taken by him, either full face or in profile, the doors of Society opened automatically. It was whispered that his name was to appear in the next Birthday Honours List ; and at the annual banquet of the Amalgamated Bulb-Squeezers, when Sir Godfrey Stooge, the retiring President, in proposing his health, concluded a glowingly eulogistic speech with the words, " Gentlemen, I give you my destined successor, Mulliner the Liberator ! " five hundred frantic photographers almost shivered the glasses on the table with their applause.

And yet he was not happy. He had lost the only girl he had ever loved, and without her what was Fame ? What was Affluence ? What were the Highest Honours in the Land ?

These were the questions he was asking

himself one night as he sat in his library, sombrely sipping a final whisky-and-soda before retiring. He had asked them once and was going to ask them again, when he was interrupted by the sound of some one ringing at the front-door bell.

He rose, surprised. It was late for callers. The domestic staff had gone to bed, so he went to the door and opened it. A shadowy figure was standing on the steps.

" Mr. Mulliner ? "

" I am Mr. Mulliner."

The man stepped past him into the hall. And, as he did so, Clarence saw that he was wearing over the upper half of his face a black velvet mask.

" I must apologise for hiding my face, Mr. Mulliner," the visitor said, as Clarence led him to the library.

" Not at all," replied Clarence, courteously. " No doubt it is all for the best."

" Indeed ? " said the other, with a touch of asperity. " If you really want to know, I am probably as handsome a man as there is in London. But my mission is one of such extraordinary secrecy that I dare not run the risk of being recognised." He paused, and

Clarence saw his eyes glint through the holes in the mask as he directed a rapid gaze into each corner of the library. " Mr. Mulliner, have you any acquaintance with the ramifications of international secret politics ? "

" I have."

" And you are a patriot ? "

" I am."

" Then I can speak freely. No doubt you are aware, Mr. Mulliner, that for some time past this country and a certain rival Power have been competing for the friendship and alliance of a certain other Power ? "

" No," said Clarence, " they didn't tell me that."

" Such is the case. And the President of this Power—— "

" Which one ? "

" The second one."

" Call it B."

" The President of Power B. is now in London. He arrived incognito, travelling under the assumed name of J. J. Shubert : and the representatives of Power A., to the best of our knowledge, are not yet aware of his presence. This gives us just the few hours necessary to clinch this treaty with

Power B. before Power A. can interfere. I ought to tell you, Mr. Mulliner, that if Power B. forms an alliance with this country, the supremacy of the Anglo-Saxon race will be secured for hundreds of years. Whereas if Power A. gets hold of Power B., civilisation will be thrown into the melting-pot. In the eyes of all Europe—and when I say all Europe I refer particularly to Powers C., D., and E. —this nation would sink to the rank of a fourth-class Power."

" Call it Power F.," said Clarence.

" It rests with you, Mr. Mulliner, to save England."

" Great Britain," corrected Clarence. He was half Scotch on his mother's side. " But how ?   What can I do about it ? "

" The position is this. The President of Power B. has an overwhelming desire to have his photograph taken by Clarence Mulliner. Consent to take it, and our difficulties will be at an end. Overcome with gratitude, he will sign the treaty, and the Anglo-Saxon race will be safe."

Clarence did not hesitate. Apart from the natural gratification of feeling that he was doing the Anglo-Saxon race a bit of

good, business was business ; and if the
President took a dozen of the large size
finished in silver wash it would mean a nice
profit.

" I shall be delighted," he said.

" Your patriotism," said the visitor, " will
not go unrewarded. It will be gratefully
noted in the Very Highest Circles."

Clarence reached for his appointment-
book.

" Now, let me see. Wednesday ?—No,
I'm full up Wednesday. Thursday ?—No.
Suppose the President looks in at my studio
between four and five on Friday ? "

The visitor uttered a gasp.

" Good heavens, Mr. Mulliner," he exclaimed, " surely you do not imagine that,
with the vast issues at stake, these things can
be done openly and in daylight ? If the
devils in the pay of Power A. were to learn
that the President intended to have his
photograph taken by you, I would not
give a straw for your chances of living an
hour."

" Then what do you suggest ? "

" You must accompany me now to the
President's suite at the Milan Hotel. We

shall travel in a closed car, and God send that these fiends did not recognise me as I came here. If they did, we shall never reach that car alive. Have you, by any chance, while we have been talking, heard the hoot of an owl ? ''

" No," said Clarence. " No owls."

" Then perhaps they are nowhere near. The fiends always imitate the hoot of an owl."

" A thing," said Clarence, " which I tried to do when I was a small boy and never seemed able to manage. The popular idea that owls say ' Tu-whit, tu-whoo ' is all wrong. The actual noise they make is something far more difficult and complex, and it was beyond me."

" Quite so." The visitor looked at his watch. " However, absorbing as these reminiscences of your boyhood days are, time is flying. Shall we be making a start ? ''

" Certainly."

" Then follow me."

It appeared to be holiday-time for fiends, or else the night-shift had not yet come on, for they reached the car without being molested. Clarence stepped in, and his masked visitor, after a keen look up and down the street, followed him.

"Talking of my boyhood——" began Clarence.

The sentence was never completed. A soft wet pad was pressed over his nostrils : the air became a-reek with the sickly fumes of chloroform : and Clarence knew no more.

When he came to, he was no longer in the car. He found himself lying on a bed in a room in a strange house. It was a medium-sized room with scarlet wall-paper, simply furnished with a wash-hand stand, a chest of drawers, two cane-bottomed chairs, and a "God Bless Our Home" motto framed in oak. He was conscious of a severe headache, and was about to rise and make for the water-bottle on the wash-stand when, to his consternation, he discovered that his arms and legs were shackled with stout cord.

As a family, the Mulliners have always been noted for their reckless courage ; and Clarence was no exception to the rule. But for an instant his heart undeniably beat a little faster. He saw now that his masked visitor had tricked him. Instead of being a representative of His Majesty's Diplomatic Service (a most respectable class of men), he had really been all along a fiend in the pay of Power A.

No doubt he and his vile associates were even now chuckling at the ease with which their victim had been duped. Clarence gritted his teeth and struggled vainly to loose the knots which secured his wrists. He had fallen back exhausted when he heard the sound of a key turning and the door opened. Somebody crossed the room and stood by the bed, looking down on him.

The new-comer was a stout man with a complexion that matched the wall-paper. He was puffing slightly, as if he had found the stairs trying. He had broad, slab-like features ; and his face was split in the middle by a walrus moustache. Somewhere and in some place, Clarence was convinced, he had seen this man before.

And then it all came back to him. An open window with a pleasant summer breeze blowing in ; a stout man in a cocked hat trying to climb through this window ; and he, Clarence, doing his best to help him with the sharp end of a tripod. It was

Jno. Horatio Biggs, the Mayor of Tooting East.

A shudder of loathing ran through Clarence.

" Traitor ! " he cried.

" Eh ? " said the Mayor.

" If anybody had told me that a son of Tooting, nursed in the keen air of freedom which blows across the Common, would sell himself for gold to the enemies of his country, I would never have believed it. Well, you may tell your employers—— "

" What employers ? "

" Power A."

" Oh, that ? " said the Mayor. " I am afraid my secretary, whom I instructed to bring you to this house, was obliged to romance a little in order to ensure your accompanying him, Mr. Mulliner. All that about Power A. and Power B. was just his little joke. If you want to know why you were brought here—— "

Clarence uttered a low groan.

" I have guessed your ghastly object, you ghastly object," he said quietly. " You want me to photograph you."

The Mayor shook his head.

" Not myself. I realise that that can never be. My daughter."

" Your daughter ? "

" My daughter."

" Does she take after you ? "

" People tell me there is a resemblance."

" I refuse," said Clarence.

" Think well, Mr. Mulliner."

" I have done all the thinking that is necessary. England—or, rather, Great Britain—looks to me to photograph only her fairest and loveliest ; and though, as a man, I admit that I loathe beautiful women, as a photographer I have a duty to consider that is higher than any personal feelings. History has yet to record an instance of a photographer playing his country false, and Clarence Mulliner is not the man to supply the first one. I decline your offer."

" I wasn't looking on it exactly as an offer," said the Mayor, thoughtfully. " More as a command, if you get my meaning."

" You imagine that you can bend a lens-artist to your will and make him false to his professional reputation ? "

" I was thinking of having a try."

" Do you realise that, if my incarcera-

tion here were known, ten thousand photographers would tear this house brick from
brick and you limb from limb ? "

" But it isn't," the Mayor pointed out.
" And that, if you follow me, is the whole
point. You came here by night in a closed
car. You could stay here for the rest of your
life, and no one would be any the wiser. I
really think you had better reconsider, Mr.
Mulliner."

" You have had my answer."

" Well, I'll leave you to think it over.
Dinner will be served at seven-thirty. Don't
bother to dress."

At half-past seven precisely the door
opened again and the Mayor reappeared,
followed by a butler bearing on a silver salver
a glass of water and a small slice of bread.
Pride urged Clarence to reject the refreshment, but hunger overcame pride. He swallowed the bread which the butler offered
him in small bits in a spoon, and drank the
water.

" At what hour would the gentleman
desire breakfast, sir ? " asked the butler.

" Now," said Clarence, for his appetite,

I

always healthy, seemed to have been sharp-
ened by the trials which he had undergone.

" Let us say nine o'clock," suggested the
Mayor. " Put aside another slice of that
bread, Meadows. And no doubt Mr. Mulliner
would enjoy a glass of this excellent water."

For perhaps half an hour after his host
had left him, Clarence's mind was obsessed
to the exclusion of all other thoughts by a
vision of the dinner he would have liked
to be enjoying. All we Mulliners have been
good trenchermen, and to put a bit of bread
into it after it had been unoccupied for a
whole day was to offer to Clarence's stomach
an insult which it resented with an inde-
scribable bitterness. Clarence's only emotion for some considerable time, then, was that
of hunger. His thoughts centred themselves
on food. And it was to this fact, oddly
enough, that he owed his release.

For, as he lay there in a sort of delirium,
picturing himself getting outside a medium-
cooked steak smothered in onions, with
grilled tomatoes and floury potatoes on the
side, it was suddenly borne in upon him that
this steak did not taste quite so good as other

steaks which he had eaten in the past. It was tough and lacked juiciness. It tasted just like rope.

And then, his mind clearing, he saw that it actually was rope. Carried away by the anguish of hunger, he had been chewing the cord which bound his hands; and he now discovered that he had bitten into it quite deeply.

A sudden flood of hope poured over Clarence Mulliner. Carrying on at this rate, he perceived, he would be able ere long to free himself. It only needed a little imagination. After a brief interval to rest his aching jaws, he put himself deliberately into that state of relaxation which is recommended by the apostles of Suggestion.

"I am entering the dining-room of my club," murmured Clarence. "I am sitting down. The waiter is handing me the bill of fare. I have selected roast duck with green peas and new potatoes, lamb cutlets with Brussels sprouts, fricassee of chicken, porterhouse steak, boiled beef and carrots, leg of mutton, haunch of mutton, mutton chops, curried mutton, veal, kidneys sauté, spaghetti Caruso, and eggs and bacon, fried on both

sides.   The waiter is now bringing my order.
I have taken up my knife and fork.   I am
beginning to eat."

And, murmuring a brief grace, Clarence
flung himself on the rope and set to.

Twenty minutes later he was hobbling
about the room, restoring the circulation
to his cramped limbs.

Just as he had succeeded in getting
himself nicely limbered up, he heard the key
turning in the door.

Clarence crouched for the spring.   The
room was quite dark now, and he was glad of
it, for darkness well fitted the work which
lay before him.   His plans, conceived on the
spur of the moment, were necessarily sketchy,
but they included jumping on the Mayor's
shoulders and pulling his head off.   After
that, no doubt, other modes of self-expression
would suggest themselves.

The door opened.   Clarence made his
leap.   And he was just about to start on the
programme as arranged, when he discovered
with a shock of horror that this was no O.B.E.
that he was being rough with, but a woman.
And no photographer worthy of the name
will ever lay a hand upon a woman, save to

raise her chin and tilt it a little more to the left.

" I beg your pardon ! " he cried.

" Don't mention it," said his visitor, in a low voice. " I hope I didn't disturb you."

" Not at all," said Clarence.

There was a pause.

" Rotten weather," said Clarence, feeling that it was for him, as the male member of the sketch, to keep the conversation going.

" Yes, isn't it ? "

" A lot of rain we've had this summer."

" Yes. It seems to get worse every year."

" Doesn't it ? "

" So bad for tennis."

" And cricket."

" And polo."

" And garden parties."

" I hate rain."

" So do I."

" Of course, we may have a fine August."

" Yes, there's always that."

The ice was broken, and the girl seemed to become more at her ease.

" I came to let you out," she said. " I must apologise for my father. He loves me foolishly and has no scruples where my happiness is concerned. He has always yearned to have me photographed by you, but I cannot consent to allow a photographer to be coerced into abandoning his principles. If you will follow me, I will let you out by the front door."

" It's awfully good of you," said Clarence, awkwardly. As any man of nice sentiment would have been, he was embarrassed. He wished that he could have obliged this kind-hearted girl by taking her picture, but a natural delicacy restrained him from touching on this subject. They went down the stairs in silence.

On the first landing a hand was placed on his in the darkness and the girl's voice whispered in his ear.

" We are just outside father's study," he heard her say. " We must be as quiet as mice."

" As what ? " said Clarence.

" Mice."

" Oh, rather," said Clarence, and immediately bumped into what appeared to be a pedestal of some sort.

These pedestals usually have vases on

top of them, and it was revealed to Clarence a moment later that this one was no exception. There was a noise like ten simultaneous dinner-services coming apart in the hands of ten simultaneous parlour-maids; and then the door was flung open, the landing became flooded with light, and the Mayor of Tooting East stood before them. He was carrying a revolver and his face was dark with menace.

" Ha ! " said the Mayor.

But Clarence was paying no attention to him. He was staring open-mouthed at the girl. She had shrunk back against the wall, and the light fell full upon her.

" You ! " cried Clarence.

" This—— " began the Mayor.

" You ! At last ! "

" This is a pretty—— "

" Am I dreaming ? "

" This is a pretty state of af—— "

" Ever since that day I saw you in the cab I have been scouring London for you. To think that I have found you at last ! "

" This is a pretty state of affairs," said the Mayor, breathing on the barrel of his revolver and polishing it on the sleeve of his coat.

" My daughter helping the foe of her family to fly—— "

" Flee, father," corrected the girl, faintly.

" Flea or fly—this is no time for arguing about insects. Let me tell you—— "

Clarence interrupted him indignantly.

" What do you mean," he cried, " by saying that she took after you ? "

" She does."

" She does not. She is the loveliest girl in the world, while you look like Lon Chaney made up for something. See for yourself." Clarence led them to the large mirror at the head of the stairs. " Your face—if you can call it that—is one of those beastly blobby squashy sort of faces—— "

" Here ! " said the Mayor.

" ——whereas hers is simply divine. Your eyes are bulbous and goofy—— "

" Hey ! " said the Mayor.

" ——while hers are sweet and soft and intelligent. Your ears—— "

" Yes, yes," said the Mayor, petulantly. " Some other time, some other time. Then am I to take it, Mr. Mulliner—— "

" Call me Clarence."

" I refuse to call you Clarence."

" You will have to very shortly, when I am your son-in-law."

The girl uttered a cry. The Mayor uttered a louder cry.

" My son-in-law ! "

" That," said Clarence, firmly, " is what I intend to be—and speedily." He turned to the girl. " I am a man of volcanic passions, and now that love has come to me there is no power in heaven or earth that can keep me from the object of my love. It will be my never-ceasing task—er——— "

" Gladys," prompted the girl.

" Thank you. It will be my never-ceasing task, Gladys, to strive daily to make you return that love——— "

" You need not strive, Clarence," she whispered, softly. " It is already returned."

Clarence reeled.

" Already ? " he gasped.

" I have loved you since I saw you in that cab. When we were torn asunder, I felt quite faint."

" So did I. I was in a daze. I tipped my cabman at Waterloo three half-crowns. I was aflame with love."

" I can hardly believe it."

I 2

"Nor could I, when I found out. I thought it was threepence. And ever since that day—— "

The Mayor coughed.

"Then am I to take it—er—Clarence," he said, " that your objections to photographing my daughter are removed ? "

Clarence laughed happily.

"Listen," he said, " and I'll show you the sort of son-in-law I am. Ruin my professional reputation though it may, I will take a photograph of you too ! "

" Me ! "

" Absolutely. Standing beside her with the tips of your fingers on her shoulder. And what's more, you can wear your cocked hat."

Tears had begun to trickle down the Mayor's cheeks.

" My boy ! " he sobbed, brokenly. " My boy ! "

And so happiness came to Clarence Mulliner at last. He never became President of the Bulb-Squeezers, for he retired from business the next day, declaring that the hand that had snapped the shutter when taking the photograph of his dear wife should never snap it again for sordid profit. The wedding, which took place some six weeks later, was attended by almost everybody of any note in Society or on the Stage ; and was the first occasion on which a bride and bride-groom had ever walked out of church beneath an arch of crossed tripods.

IX

HONEYSUCKLE COTTAGE

"DO you believe in ghosts?" asked Mr. Mulliner abruptly.

I weighed the question thoughtfully. I was a little surprised, for nothing in our previous conversation had suggested the topic.

"Well," I replied, "I don't like them, if that's what you mean. I was once butted by one as a child."

"Ghosts. Not goats."

"Oh, ghosts? Do I believe in ghosts?"

"Exactly."

"Well, yes—and no."

"Let me put it another way," said Mr. Mulliner, patiently. "Do you believe in haunted houses? Do you believe that it is possible for a malign influence to envelop a place and work a spell on all who come within its radius?"

I hesitated.

" Well, no—and yes."

Mr. Mulliner sighed a little. He seemed to be wondering if I was always as bright as this.

" Of course," I went on, " one has read stories. Henry James's *Turn of The Screw* . . ."

" I am not talking about fiction."

" Well, in real life—— Well, look here, I once, as a matter of fact, did meet a man who knew a fellow . . ."

" My distant cousin James Rodman spent some weeks in a haunted house," said Mr. Mulliner, who, if he has a fault, is not a very good listener. " It cost him five thousand pounds. That is to say, he sacrificed five thousand pounds by not remaining there. Did you ever," he asked, wandering, it seemed to me, from the subject, " hear of Leila J. Pinckney ?'

Naturally I had heard of Leila J. Pinckney. Her death some years ago has diminished her vogue, but at one time it was impossible to pass a book-shop or a railway bookstall without seeing a long row of her novels. I had never myself actually read any of them, but I knew that in her particular line of literature, the Squashily Sentimental, she had always been regarded by those entitled to judge as pre-eminent. The critics usually headed their reviews of her stories with the words :—

ANOTHER PINCKNEY

or sometimes, more offensively :—

ANOTHER PINCKNEY ! ! !

And once, dealing with, I think, *The Love Which Prevails*, the literary expert of the *Scrutinizer* had compressed his entire critique into the single phrase " Oh, God ! "

" Of course," I said. " But what about her ? "

" She was James Rodman's aunt."

" Yes ? "

" And when she died James found that she had left him five thousand pounds and the house in the country where she had lived for the last twenty years of her life."

" A very nice little legacy."

" Twenty years," repeated Mr. Mulliner. " Grasp that, for it has a vital bearing on what follows. Twenty years, mind you, and

Miss Pinckney turned out two novels and twelve short stories regularly every year, besides a monthly page of Advice to Young Girls in one of the magazines. That is to say, forty of her novels and no fewer than two hundred and forty of her short stories were written under the roof of Honeysuckle Cottage."

" A pretty name." .

" A nasty, sloppy name," said Mr. Mulliner severely, " which should have warned my distant cousin James from the start. Have you a pencil and a piece of paper ? " He scribbled for awhile, poring frowningly over columns of figures. " Yes," he said, looking up, " if my calculations are correct, Leila J. Pinckney wrote in all a matter of nine million one hundred and forty thousand words of glutinous sentimentality at Honey-suckle Cottage, and it was a condition of her will that James should reside there for six months in every year. Failing to do this, he was to forfeit the five thousand pounds."

" It must be great fun making a freak will," I mused. " I often wish I was rich enough to do it."

" This was not a freak will. The con-

ditions are perfectly understandable. James
Rodman was a writer of sensational mystery
stories, and his aunt Leila had always dis-
approved of his work. She was a great
believer in the influence of environment, and
the reason why she inserted that clause in
her will was that she wished to compel James
to move from London to the country. She
considered that living in London hardened
him and made his outlook on life sordid. She
often asked him if he thought it quite nice to
harp so much on sudden death and blackmailers with squints. Surely, she said, there
were enough squinting blackmailers in the
world without writing about them.

"The fact that Literature meant such
different things to these two had, I believe,
caused something of a coolness between them,
and James had never dreamed that he would
be remembered in his aunt's will. For he
had never concealed his opinion that Leila
J. Pinckney's style of writing revolted him,
however dear it might be to her enormous
public. He held rigid views on the art of
the novel, and always maintained that an
artist with a true reverence for his craft
should not descend to goo-ey love stories,

but should stick austerely to revolvers, cries in the night, missing papers, mysterious Chinamen and dead bodies—with or without gash in throat. And not even the thought that his aunt had dandled him on her knee as a baby could induce him to stifle his literary conscience to the extent of pretending to enjoy her work. First, last and all the time, James Rodman had held the opinion—and voiced it fearlessly—that Leila J. Pinckney wrote bilge.

" It was a surprise to him, therefore, to find that he had been left this legacy. A pleasant surprise, of course. James was making quite a decent income out of the three novels and eighteen short stories which he produced annually, but an author can always find a use for five thousand pounds. And, as for the cottage, he had actually been looking about for a little place in the country at the very moment when he received the lawyer's letter. In less than a week he was installed at his new residence."

James's first impressions of Honeysuckle Cottage were, he tells me, wholly favourable. He was delighted with the place. It was a low, rambling, picturesque old house with funny little chimneys and a red roof, placed in the middle of the most charming country. With its oak beams, its trim garden, its trilling birds and its rose-hung porch, it was the ideal spot for a writer. It was just the sort of place, he reflected whimsically, which his aunt had loved to write about in her books. Even the apple-cheeked old housekeeper who attended to his needs might have stepped straight out of one of them.

It seemed to James that his lot had been cast in pleasant places. He had brought down his books, his pipes and his golf clubs, and was hard at work finishing the best thing he had ever done. *The Secret Nine* was the title of it ; and on the beautiful summer afternoon on which this story opens he was in the study, hammering away at his typewriter, at peace with the world. The machine was running sweetly, the new tobacco he had bought the day before was proving admirable, and he was moving on all six cylinders to the end of a chapter.

He shoved in a fresh sheet of paper, chewed his pipe thoughtfully for a moment, then wrote rapidly :

" For an instant Lester Gage thought that he must have been mistaken. Then the noise came again, faint but unmistakable —a soft scratching on the outer panel.

" His mouth set in a grim line. Silently, like a panther, he made one quick step to the desk, noiselessly opened a drawer, drew out his automatic. After that affair of the poisoned needle, he was taking no chances. Still in dead silence, he tiptoed to the door ; then, flinging it suddenly open, he stood there, his weapon poised.

" On the mat stood the most beautiful girl he had ever beheld. A veritable child of Faërie. She eyed him for a moment with a saucy smile ; then with a pretty, roguish look of reproof shook a dainty fore-finger at him.

" ' I believe you've forgotten me, Mr. Gage ! ' she fluted with a mock severity which her eyes belied."

James stared at the paper dumbly. He was utterly perplexed. He had not had the slightest intention of writing anything like this. To begin with, it was a rule with him, and one which he never broke, to allow no girls to appear in his stories. Sinister landladies, yes, and naturally any amount of adventuresses with foreign accents, but never under any pretext what may be broadly described as girls. A detective story, he maintained, should have no heroine. Heroines only held up the action and tried to flirt with the hero when he should have been busy looking for clues, and then went and let the villain kidnap them by some childishly simple trick. In his writing, James was positively monastic.

And yet here was this creature with her saucy smile and her dainty forefinger horning in at the most important point in the story. It was uncanny.

He looked once more at his scenario. No, the scenario was all right.

In perfectly plain words it stated that what happened when the door opened was that a dying man fell in and after gasping, "The beetle! Tell Scotland Yard that the blue beetle is——" expired on the hearth-rug, leaving Lester Gage not unnaturally somewhat mystified. Nothing whatever about any beautiful girls.

In a curious mood of irritation, James scratched out the offending passage, wrote in the necessary corrections and put the cover on the machine. It was at this point that he heard William whining.

The only blot on this paradise which James had so far been able to discover was the infernal dog, William. Belonging nominally to the gardener, on the very first morning he had adopted James by acclamation, and he maddened and infuriated James. He had a habit of coming and whining under the window when James was at work. The latter would ignore this as long as he could ; then, when the thing became insupportable, would bound out of his chair, to see the animal standing on the gravel, gazing expectantly up at him with a stone in his mouth. William had a weak-minded passion for chasing stones ; and on the first day James, in a rash spirit of camaraderie, had flung one for him. Since then James had thrown no more stones ; but he had thrown any number of other solids, and the garden was littered with objects ranging from match boxes to a plaster statuette of the young Joseph prophesying before Pharaoh. And still William came and whined, an optimist to the last.

The whining, coming now at a moment when he felt irritable and unsettled, acted on James much as the scratching on the door had acted on Lester Gage. Silently, like a panther, he made one quick step to the mantelpiece, removed from it a china mug bearing the legend A Present From Clacton-on-Sea, and crept to the window.

And as he did so a voice outside said, " Go away, sir, go away ! " and there followed a short, high-pitched bark which was certainly not William's. William was a mixture of Airedale, setter, bull terrier, and mastiff ; and when in vocal mood, favoured the mastiff side of his family.

James peered out. There on the porch stood a girl in blue. She held in her arms a small fluffy white dog, and she was endeavouring to foil the upward movement toward this of the blackguard William. William's mentality had been arrested some years before at the point where he imagined that everything in the world had been created for him to eat. A bone, a boot, a steak, the back wheel of a bicycle—it was all one to William. If it was there he tried to eat it. He had even made a plucky attempt to devour the remains of the young Joseph prophesying before Pharaoh. And it was perfectly plain now that he regarded the curious wriggling object in the girl's arms purely in the light of a snack to keep body and soul together till dinner-time.

" William ! " bellowed James.

William looked courteously over his shoulder with eyes that beamed with the pure light of a life's devotion, wagged the whiplike tail which he had inherited from his bull-terrier ancestor and resumed his intent scrutiny of the fluffy dog.

" Oh, please ! " cried the girl. " This great rough dog is frightening poor Toto."

The man of letters and the man of action do not always go hand in hand, but practice had made James perfect in handling with a swift efficiency any situation that involved William. A moment later that canine moron, having received the present from Clacton in the short ribs, was scuttling round the corner of the house, and James had jumped through the window and was facing the girl.

She was an extraordinarily pretty girl Very sweet and fragile she looked as she stood there under the honeysuckle with the breeze ruffling a tendril of golden hair that strayed from beneath her coquettish little hat. Her eyes were very big and very blue, her rose-tinted face becomingly flushed. All wasted on James, though. He disliked all girls, and particularly the sweet, droopy type.

" Did you want to see somebody ? " he asked stiffly.

" Just the house," said the girl, " if it wouldn't be giving any trouble. I do so want to see the room where Miss Pinckney wrote her books. This is where Leila J. Pinckney used to live, isn't it ? "

" Yes ; I am her nephew. My name is James Rodman."

" Mine is Rose Maynard."

James led the way into the house, and she stopped with a cry of delight on the threshold of the morning room.

" Oh, how too perfect ! " she cried. " So this was her study ? "

" Yes."

" What a wonderful place it would be for you to think in if you were a writer too."

James held no high opinion of women's literary taste, but nevertheless he was conscious of an unpleasant shock.

" I am a writer," he said coldly. " I write detective stories."

" I—I'm afraid "—she blushed—" I'm afraid I don't often read detective stories."

" You no doubt prefer," said James, still more coldly, " the sort of thing my aunt used to write."

" Oh, I love her stories ! " cried the girl, clasping her hands ecstatically. "Don't you?"

" I cannot say that I do."

" What ? "

" They are pure apple sauce," said James sternly ; " just nasty blobs of sentimentality, thoroughly untrue to life."

The girl stared.

" Why, that's just what's so wonderful about them, their trueness to life! You feel they might all have happened. I don't understand what you mean."

They were walking down the garden now. James held the gate open for her and she passed through into the road.

" Well, for one thing," he said, " I decline to believe that a marriage between two young people is invariably preceded by some violent and sensational experience in which they both share."

" Are you thinking of *Scent o' the Blossom*, where Edgar saves Maud from drowning ? "

" I am thinking of every single one of my aunt's books." He looked at her curiously. He had just got the solution of a mystery which had been puzzling him for some time. Almost from the moment he had set eyes on her she had seemed somehow strangely familiar. It now suddenly came to him why it was that he disliked her so much. " Do you know," he said, " you might be one of my aunt's heroines yourself ? You're just the sort of girl she used to love to write about."

Her face lit up.

" Oh, do you really think so ? " She hesitated. " Do you know what I have been feeling ever since I came here ? I've been feeling that you are exactly like one of Miss Pinckney's heroes."

" No, I say, really ! " said James, revolted.

" Oh, but you are ! When you jumped through that window it gave me quite a start. You were so exactly like Claude Masterson in *Heather o' the Hills*."

" I have not read *Heather o' the Hills*," said James, with a shudder.

" He was very strong and quiet, with deep, dark, sad eyes."

James did not explain that his eyes were sad becáuse her society gave him a pain in the neck. He merely laughed scornfully.

" So now, I suppose," he said, " a car will come and knock you down and I shall carry you gently into the house and lay you—— Look out ! " he cried.

It was too late. She was lying in a little huddled heap at his feet. Round the corner a large automobile had come bowling, keeping with an almost affected precision to the wrong side of the road. It was now receding into the distance, the occupant of the tonneau, a stout red-faced gentleman in a fur coat, leaning out over the back. He had bared his head—not, one fears, as a pretty gesture of respect and regret, but because he was using his hat to hide the number plate.

The dog Toto was unfortunately uninjured.

James carried the girl gently into the house and laid her on the sofa in the morning-room. He rang the bell and the apple-cheeked housekeeper appeared.

" Send for the doctor," said James. " There has been an accident."

The housekeeper bent over the girl.

" Eh, dearie, dearie ! " she said. " Bless her sweet pretty face ! "

The gardener, he who technically owned William, was routed out from among the young lettuces and told to fetch Doctor Brady. He separated his bicycle from William, who was making a light meal off the left pedal, and departed on his mission. Doctor Brady arrived and in due course he made his report.

" No bones broken, but a number of nasty bruises. And, of course, the shock. She will have to stay here for some time, Rodman. Can't be moved."

" Stay here ! But she can't ! It isn't proper."

" Your housekeeper will act as a chaperon."

The doctor sighed. He was a stolid-looking man of middle age with side whiskers.

" A beautiful girl, that, Rodman," he said.

" I suppose so," said James.

" A sweet, beautiful girl. An elfin child."

" A what ? " cried James, starting.

This imagery was very foreign to Doctor Brady as he knew him. On the only previous occasion on which they had had any extended conversation, the doctor had talked exclusively about the effect of too much protein on the gastric juices.

" An elfin child ; a tender, fairy creature. When I was looking at her just now, Rodman, I nearly broke down. Her little hand lay on the coverlet like some white lily floating on the surface of a still pool, and her dear, trusting eyes gazed up at me."

He pottered off down the garden, still babbling, and James stood staring after him blankly. And slowly, like some cloud athwart a summer sky, there crept over James's heart the chill shadow of a nameless fear.

It was about a week later that Mr. Andrew McKinnon, the senior partner in the well-known firm of literary agents, McKinnon & Gooch, sat in his office in Chancery Lane, frowning thoughtfully over a telegram. He rang the bell.

" Ask Mr. Gooch to step in here." He

resumed his study of the telegram. " Oh, Gooch," he said when his partner appeared, " I've just had a curious wire from young Rodman. He seems to want to see me very urgently."

Mr. Gooch read the telegram.

" Written under the influence of some strong mental excitement," he agreed. " I wonder why he doesn't come to the office if he wants to see you so badly."

" He's working very hard, finishing that novel for Prodder & Wiggs. Can't leave it, I suppose. Well, it's a nice day. If you will look after things here I think I'll motor down and let him give me lunch."

As Mr. McKinnon's car reached the crossroads a mile from Honeysuckle Cottage, he was aware of a gesticulating figure by the hedge. He stopped the car.

" Morning, Rodman."

" Thank God, you've come ! " said James. It seemed to Mr. McKinnon that the young man looked paler and thinner. " Would you mind walking the rest of the way ? There's something I want to speak to you about."

Mr. McKinnon alighted ; and James, as

he glanced at him, felt cheered and encouraged by the very sight of the man. The literary agent was a grim, hard-bitten person, to whom, when he called at their offices to arrange terms, editors kept their faces turned so that they might at least retain their back collar studs. There was no sentiment in Andrew McKinnon. Editresses of society papers practised their blandishments on him in vain, and many a publisher had waked screaming in the night, dreaming that he was signing a McKinnon contract.

" Well, Rodman," he said, " Prodder & Wiggs have agreed to our terms. I was writing to tell you so when your wire arrived. I had a lot of trouble with them, but it's fixed at 20 per cent., rising to 25, and two hundred pounds advance royalties on day of publication."

" Good ! " said James absently. " Good ! McKinnon, do you remember my aunt, Leila J. Pinckney ? "

" Remember her ? Why, I was her agent all her life."

" Of course. Then you know the sort of tripe she wrote."

" No author," said Mr. McKinnon reprovingly, " who pulls down a steady twenty thousand pounds a year writes tripe."

" Well anyway, you know her stuff."

" Who better ? "

" When she died she left me five thousand pounds and her house, Honeysuckle Cottage. I'm living there now. McKinnon, do you believe in haunted houses ? "

" No."

" Yet I tell you solemnly that Honeysuckle Cottage is haunted ! "

" By your aunt ? " said Mr. McKinnon, surprised.

" By her influence. There's a malignant spell over the place ; a sort of miasma of sentimentalism. Everybody who enters it succumbs."

" Tut-tut ! You mustn't have these fancies."

" They aren't fancies."

" You aren't seriously meaning to tell me—— "

" Well, how do you account for this ? That book you were speaking about, which Prodder & Wiggs are to publish—*The Secret Nine*. Every time I sit down to write it a girl keeps trying to sneak in."

" Into the room ? "

" Into the story."

" You don't want a love interest in your sort of book," said Mr. McKinnon, shaking his head. " It delays the action."

" I know it does. And every day I have to keep shooing this infernal female out. An awful girl, McKinnon. A soppy, soupy, treacly, drooping girl with a roguish smile. This morning she tried to butt in on the scene where Lester Gage is trapped in the den of the mysterious leper."

" No ! "

" She did, I assure you. I had to rewrite three pages before I could get her out of it. And that's not the worst. Do you know, McKinnon, that at this moment I am actually living the plot of a typical Leila May Pinckney novel in just the setting she always used ! And I can see the happy ending coming nearer every day ! A week ago a girl was knocked down by a car at my door and I've had to put her up, and every day I realise more clearly that sooner or later I shall ask her to marry me."

" Don't do it," said Mr. McKinnon, a stout bachelor. " You're too young to marry."

K

"So was Methuselah," said James, a stouter. "But all the same I know I'm going to do it. It's the influence of this awful house weighing upon me. I feel like an eggshell in a maelstrom. I am being sucked on by a force too strong for me to resist. This morning I found myself kissing her dog!"

"No!"

"I did! And I loathe the little beast. Yesterday I got up at dawn and plucked a nosegay of flowers for her, wet with the dew."

"Rodman!"

"It's a fact. I laid them at her door and went downstairs kicking myself all the way. And there in the hall was the apple-cheeked housekeeper regarding me archly. If she didn't murmur ' Bless their sweet young hearts!' my ears deceived me."

"Why don't you pack up and leave?"

"If I do I lose the five thousand pounds."

"Ah!" said Mr. McKinnon.

"I can understand what has happened. It's the same with all haunted houses. My aunt's subliminal ether vibrations have woven themselves into the texture of the place, creating an atmosphere which forces the

ego of all who come in contact with it to
attune themselves to it.   It's either that or
something to do with the fourth dimension."

Mr. McKinnon laughed scornfully.

" Tut-tut ! " he said again.   " This is
pure imagination.   What has happened is
that you've been working too hard.   You'll
see this precious atmosphere of yours will
have no effect on me."

" That's exactly why I asked you to
come down.   I hoped you might break the
spell."

" I will that," said Mr. McKinnon jovially.

The fact that the literary agent spoke
little at lunch caused James no apprehension.
Mr. McKinnon was ever a silent trencherman.
From time to time James caught him stealing
a glance at the girl, who was well enough to
come down to meals now, limping pathetic-
ally ; but he could read nothing in his face.
And yet the mere look of his face was a consolation.   It was so solid, so matter of fact,
so exactly like an unemotional coconut.

" You've done me good," said James
with a sigh of relief, as he escorted the agent
down the garden to his car after lunch.
" I felt all along that I could rely on your

rugged common sense. The whole atmosphere of the place seems different now."

Mr. McKinnon did not speak for a moment. He seemed to be plunged in thought.

" Rodman," he said, as he got into his car, " I've been thinking over that suggestion of yours of putting a love interest into *The Secret Nine*. I think you're wise. The story needs it. After all, what is there greater in the world than love ? Love— love—aye, it's the sweetest word in the language. Put in a heroine and let her marry Lester Gage."

" If," said James grimly, " she does succeed in worming her way in she'll jolly well marry the mysterious leper. But look here, I don't understand—— "

" It was seeing that girl that changed me," proceeded Mr. McKinnon. And as James stared at him aghast, tears suddenly filled his hard-boiled eyes. He openly snuffled. " Aye, seeing her sitting there under the roses, with all that smell of honeysuckle and all. And the birdies singing so sweet in the garden and the sun lighting up her bonny face. The puir wee lass ! " he muttered, dabbing at his eyes. " The puir

bonny wee lass! Rodman," he said, his
voice quivering, "I've decided that we're
being hard on Prodder & Wiggs. Wiggs has
had sickness in his home lately. We mustn't
be hard on a man who's had sickness in his
home, hey, laddie? No, no! I'm going to
take back that contract and alter it to a
flat 12 per cent. and no advance royalties."

"What!"

"But you shan't lose by it, Rodman.
No, no, you shan't lose by it, my manny.
I am going to waive my commission. The
puir bonny wee lass!"

The car rolled off down the road. Mr.
McKinnon, seated in the back, was blowing
his nose violently.

"This is the end!" said James.

It is necessary at this point to pause and
examine James Rodman's position with an
unbiassed eye. The average man, unless he
puts himself in James's place, will be unable
to appreciate it. James, he will feel, was
making a lot of fuss about nothing. Here he
was, drawing daily closer and closer to a
charming girl with big blue eyes, and surely
rather to be envied than pitied.

But we must remember that James was one of Nature's bachelors. And no ordinary man, looking forward dreamily to a little home of his own with a loving wife putting out his slippers and changing the gramophone records, can realise the intensity of the instinct for self-preservation which animates Nature's bachelors in times of peril.

James Rodman had a congenital horror of matrimony. Though a young man, he had allowed himself to develop a great many habits which were as the breath of life to him; and these habits, he knew instinctively, a wife would shoot to pieces within a week of the end of the honeymoon.

James liked to breakfast in bed; and, having breakfasted, to smoke in bed and knock the ashes out on the carpet. What wife would tolerate this practice?

James liked to pass his days in a tennis shirt, gray flannel trousers and slippers. What wife ever rests until she has inclosed her husband in a stiff collar, tight boots and a morning suit and taken him with her to *thés musicales?*

These and a thousand other thoughts of the same kind flashed through the unfortunate young man's mind as the days went by, and every day that passed seemed to draw him nearer to the brink of the chasm. Fate appeared to be taking a malicious pleasure in making things as difficult for him as possible. Now that the girl was well enough to leave her bed, she spent her time sitting in a chair on the sun-sprinkled porch, and James had to read to her—and poetry, at that ; and not the jolly, wholesome sort of poetry the boys are turning out nowadays, either—good, honest stuff about sin and gas works and decaying corpses—but the old-fashioned kind with rhymes in it, dealing almost exclusively with love. The weather, moreover, continued superb. The honeysuckle cast its sweet scent on the gentle breeze ; the roses over the porch stirred and nodded ; the flowers in the garden were lovelier than ever ; the birds sang their little throats sore. And every evening there was a magnificent sunset. It was almost as if Nature were doing it on purpose.

At last James intercepted Doctor Brady as he was leaving after one of his visits and put the thing to him squarely :

" When is that girl going ? "

The doctor patted him on the arm.

"Not yet, Rodman," he said in a low, understanding voice. "No need to worry yourself about that. Mustn't be moved for days and days and days—I might almost say weeks and weeks and weeks."

"Weeks and weeks!" cried James.

"And weeks," said Doctor Brady. He prodded James roguishly in the abdomen. "Good luck to you, my boy, good luck to you," he said.

It was some small consolation to James that the mushy physician immediately afterward tripped over William on his way down the path and broke his stethoscope. When a man is up against it like James every little helps.

He was walking dismally back to the house after this conversation when he was met by the apple-cheeked housekeeper.

"The little lady would like to speak to you, sir," said the apple-cheeked exhibit, rubbing her hands.

"Would she?" said James hollowly.

"So sweet and pretty she looks, sir—oh, sir, you wouldn't believe! Like a blessed angel sitting there with her dear eyes all a-shining."

"Don't do it!" cried James with extraordinary vehemence. "Don't do it!"

He found the girl propped up on the cushions and thought once again how singularly he disliked her. And yet, even as he thought this, some force against which he had to fight madly was whispering to him, "Go to her and take that little hand! Breathe into that little ear the burning words that will make that little face turn away crimsoned with blushes!" He wiped a bead of perspiration from his forehead and sat down.

"Mrs. Stick-in-the-Mud—what's her name?—says you want to see me."

The girl nodded.

"I've had a letter from Uncle Henry. I wrote to him as soon as I was better and told him what had happened, and he is coming here to-morrow morning."

"Uncle Henry?"

"That's what I call him, but he's really no relation. He is my guardian. He and daddy were officers in the same regiment, and when daddy was killed, fighting on the

K 2

Afghan frontier, he died in Uncle Henry's arms and with his last breath begged him to take care of me."

James started. A sudden wild hope had waked in his heart. Years ago, he remembered, he had read a book of his aunt's entitled *Rupert's Legacy*, and in that book——

" I'm engaged to marry him," said the girl quietly.

" Wow ! " shouted James.

" What ? " asked the girl, startled.

" Touch of cramp," said James. He was thrilling all over. That wild hope had been realised.

" It was daddy's dying wish that we should marry," said the girl.

" And dashed sensible of him, too ; dashed sensible," said James warmly.

" And yet," she went on, a little wistfully, " I sometimes wonder—— "

" Don't ! " said James. " Don't ! You must respect daddy's dying wish. There's nothing like daddy's dying wish ; you can't beat it. So he's coming here to-morrow, is he ? Capital, capital ! To lunch, I suppose ? Excellent ! I'll run down and tell Mrs. Who-Is-It to lay in another chop."

It was with a gay and uplifted heart that James strolled the garden and smoked his pipe next morning. A great cloud seemed to have rolled itself away from him. Everything was for the best in the best of all possible worlds. He had finished *The Secret Nine* and shipped it off to Mr. McKinnon, and now as he strolled there was shaping itself in his mind a corking plot about a man with only half a face who lived in a secret den and terrorised London with a series of shocking murders. And what made them so shocking was the fact that each of the victims, when discovered, was found to have only half a face too. The rest had been chipped off, presumably by some blunt instrument.

The thing was coming out magnificently, when suddenly his attention was diverted by a piercing scream. Out of the bushes fringing the river that ran beside the garden burst the apple-cheeked housekeeper.

" Oh, sir ! Oh, sir ! Oh, sir ! "

" What is it ? " demanded James irritably.

" Oh, sir ! Oh, sir ! Oh, sir ! "

" Yes, and then what ? "

"The little dog, sir! He's in the river!"

"Well, whistle him to come out."

"Oh, sir, do come quick! He'll be drowned!"

James followed her through the bushes, taking off his coat as he went. He was saying to himself, "I will not rescue this dog. I do not like the dog. It is high time he had a bath, and in any case it would be much simpler to stand on the bank and fish for him with a rake. Only an ass out of a Leila J. Pinckney book would dive into a beastly river to save——"

At this point he dived. Toto, alarmed by the splash, swam rapidly for the bank, but James was too quick for him. Grasping him firmly by the neck, he scrambled ashore and ran for the house, followed by the housekeeper.

The girl was seated on the porch. Over her there bent the tall soldierly figure of a man with keen eyes and graying hair. The housekeeper raced up.

"Oh, miss! Toto! In the river! He saved him! He plunged in and saved him!"

The girl drew a quick breath.

"Gallant, damme! By Jove! By gad!

Yes, gallant, by George ! '' exclaimed the soldierly man.

The girl seemed to wake from a reverie.

" Uncle Henry, this is Mr. Rodman. Mr. Rodman, my guardian, Colonel Carteret."

" Proud to meet you, sir," said the colonel, his honest blue eyes glowing as he fingered his short crisp moustache. " As fine a thing as I ever heard of, damme ! ''

" Yes, you are brave—brave," the girl whispered.

" I am wet—wet," said James, and went upstairs to change his clothes.

When he came down for lunch, he found to his relief that the girl had decided not to join them, and Colonel Carteret was silent and preoccupied. James, exerting himself in his capacity of host, tried him with the weather, golf, India, the Government, the high cost of living, first-class cricket, the modern dancing craze, and murderers he had met, but the other still preserved that strange, absent-minded silence. It was only when the meal was concluded and James had produced cigarettes that he came abruptly out of his trance.

"Rodman," he said, "I should like to speak to you."

"Yes?" said James, thinking it was about time.

"Rodman," said Colonel Carteret, "or rather, George—I may call you George?" he added, with a sort of wistful diffidence that had a singular charm.

"Certainly," replied James, "if you wish it. Though my name is James."

"James, eh? Well, well, it amounts to the same thing, eh, what, damme, by gad?" said the colonel with a momentary return of his bluff soldierly manner. "Well, then, James, I have something that I wish to say to you. Did Miss Maynard—did Rose happen to tell you anything about myself in—er—in connection with herself?"

"She mentioned that you and she were engaged to be married."

The colonel's tightly drawn lips quivered.

"No longer," he said.

"What?"

"No, John, my boy."

"James."

"No, James, my boy, no longer. While you were upstairs changing your clothes she told me—breaking down, poor child, as she spoke—that she wished our engagement to be at an end."

James half rose from the table, his cheeks blanched.

" You don't mean that ! " he gasped.

Colonel Carteret nodded.   He was staring out of the window, his fine eyes set in a look of pain.

" But this is nonsense ! " cried James. " This is absurd !   She—she mustn't be allowed to chop and change like this.   I mean to say, it—it isn't fair—— "

" Don't think of me, my boy."

" I'm not—I mean, did she give any reason ? "

" Her eyes did."

" Her eyes did ? "

" Her eyes, when she looked at you on the porch, as you stood there—young, heroic —having just saved the life of the dog she loves.   It is you who have won that tender heart, my boy."

" Now listen," protested James, " you aren't going to sit there and tell me that a girl falls in love with a man just because he saves her dog from drowning ? "

"Why, surely," said Colonel Carteret surprised. "What better reason could she have?" He sighed. "It is the old, old story, my boy. Youth to youth. I am an old man. I should have known—I should have foreseen—yes, youth to youth."

"You aren't a bit old."

"Yes, yes."

"No, no."

"Yes, yes."

"Don't keep on saying yes, yes!" cried James, clutching at his hair. "Besides, she wants a steady old buffer—a steady, sensible man of medium age—to look after her."

Colonel Carteret shook his head with a gentle smile.

"This is mere quixotry, my boy. It is splendid of you to take this attitude; but no, no."

"Yes, yes."

"No, no." He gripped James's hand for an instant, then rose and walked to the door. "That is all I wished to say, Tom."

"James."

"James. I just thought that you ought to know how matters stood. Go to her, my

boy, go to her, and don't let any thought of
an old man's broken dream keep you from
pouring out what is in your heart. I am an
old soldier, lad, an old soldier. I have
learned to take the rough with the smooth.
But I think—I think I will leave you now.
I—I should—should like to be alone for a
while. If you need me you will find me in
the raspberry bushes."

He had scarcely gone when James also
left the room. He took his hat and stick
and walked blindly out of the garden, he
knew not whither. His brain was numbed.
Then, as his powers of reasoning returned,
he told himself that he should have foreseen this ghastly thing. If there was one
type of character over which Leila J. Pinckney
had been wont to spread herself, it was the
pathetic guardian who loves his ward but
relinquishes her to the younger man. No
wonder the girl had broken off the engagement. Any elderly guardian who allowed
himself to come within a mile of Honeysuckle
Cottage was simply asking for it. And
then, as he turned to walk back, a sort of dull
defiance gripped James. Why, he asked,
should he be put upon in this manner? If

the girl liked to throw over this man, why should he be the goat ?

He saw his way clearly now. He just wouldn't do it, that was all. And if they didn't like it they could lump it.

Full of a new fortitude, he strode in at the gate. A tall, soldierly figure emerged from the raspberry bushes and came to meet him.

" Well ? " said Colonel Carteret.

" Well ? " said James defiantly.

" Am I to congratulate you ? "

James caught his keen blue eye and hesitated. It was not going to be so simple as he had supposed.

" Well—er—— " he said.

Into the keen blue eyes there came a look that James had not seen there before. It was the stern, hard look which—probably—had caused men to bestow upon this old soldier the name of Cold-Steel Carteret.

" You have not asked Rose to marry you ? "

" Er—no ; not yet."

The keen blue eyes grew keener and bluer.

" Rodman," said Colonel Carteret in a strange, quiet voice, " I have known that little girl since she was a tiny child. For years she has been all in all to me. Her father died in my arms and with his last breath bade me see that no harm came to his darling. I have nursed her through mumps, measles—aye, and chicken pox— and I live but for her happiness." He paused, with a significance that made James's toes curl. "Rodman," he said, "do you know what I would do to any man who trifled with that little girl's affections?" He reached in his hip pocket and an ugly-looking revolver glittered in the sunlight. "I would shoot him like a dog."

"Like a dog?" faltered James.

"Like a dog," said Colonel Carteret. He took James's arm and turned him toward the house. "She is on the porch. Go to her. And if——" He broke off. "But tut!" he said in a kindlier tone. "I am doing you an injustice, my boy. I know it."

"Oh, you are," said James fervently.

"Your heart is in the right place."

"Oh, absolutely," said James."

"Then go to her, my boy. Later on you may have something to tell me. You will find me in the strawberry beds."

It was very cool and fragrant on the porch. Overhead, little breezes played and laughed among the roses. Somewhere in the distance sheep bells tinkled, and in the shrubbery a thrush was singing its even-song.

Seated in her chair behind a wicker table laden with tea things, Rose Maynard watched James as he shambled up the path.

" Tea's ready," she called gaily. " Where is Uncle Henry ? " A look of pity and dis-tress flitted for a moment over her flower-like face. " Oh, I—I forgot," she whispered.

" He is in the strawberry beds," said James in a low voice.

She nodded unhappily.

" Of course, of course. Oh, why is life like this ? " James heard her whisper.

He sat down. He looked at the girl. She was leaning back with closed eyes, and he thought he had never seen such a little squirt in his life. The idea of passing his remaining days in her society revolted him. He was stoutly opposed to the idea of marry-ing anyone ; but if, as happens to the best of us, he ever were compelled to perform the wedding glide, he had always hoped it would be with some lady golf champion who would help him with his putting, and thus, by bringing his handicap down a notch or two, enable him to save something from the wreck, so to speak. But to link his lot with a girl who read his aunt's books and liked them ; a girl who could tolerate the presence of the dog Toto ; a girl who clasped her hands in pretty, childish joy when she saw a nasturtium in bloom—it was too much. Nevertheless, he took her hand and began to speak.

" Miss Maynard—Rose——— "

She opened her eyes and cast them down. A flush had come into her cheeks. The dog Toto at her side sat up and begged for cake, disregarded.

" Let me tell you a story. Once upon a time there was a lonely man who lived in a cottage all by himself——— "

He stopped. Was it James Rodman who was talking this bilge ?

" Yes ? " whispered the girl.

" ———but one day there came to him out of nowhere a little fairy princess. She——— "

He stopped again, but this time not because of the sheer shame of listening to his own voice. What caused him to interrupt his tale was the fact that at this moment the tea table suddenly began to rise slowly in the air, tilting as it did so a considerable quantity of hot tea on to the knees of his trousers.

" Ouch ! " cried James, leaping.

The table continued to rise, and then fell sideways, revealing the homely countenance of William, who, concealed by the cloth, had been taking a nap beneath it. He moved slowly forward, his eyes on Toto. For many a long day William had been desirous of putting to the test, once and for all, the problem of whether Toto was edible or not. Sometimes he thought yes, at other times no. Now seemed an admirable opportunity for a definite decision. He advanced on the object of his experiment, making a low whistling noise through his nostrils, not unlike a boiling kettle. And Toto, after one long look of incredulous horror, tucked his shapely tail between his legs and, turning, raced for safety. He had laid a course in a bee line for the open garden gate, and William, shaking a dish of marmalade off his head a little petulantly, galloped ponderously after him. Rose Maynard staggered to her feet.

" Oh, save him ! " she cried.

Without a word James added himself to the procession. His interest in Toto was but tepid. What he wanted was to get near enough to William to discuss with him that matter of the tea on his trousers. He reached the road and found that the order of the runners had not changed. For so small a dog, Toto was moving magnificently. A cloud of dust rose as he skidded round the corner. William followed. James followed William.

And so they passed Farmer Birkett's barn, Farmer Giles' cow shed, the place where Farmer Willetts' pigsty used to be before the big fire, and the Bunch of Grapes public house, Jno. Biggs propr., licensed to sell tobacco, wines and spirits. And it was as they were turning down the lane that leads past Farmer Robinson's chicken run that Toto, thinking swiftly, bolted abruptly into a small drain pipe.

" William ! " roared James, coming up at a canter. He stopped to pluck a branch from the hedge and swooped darkly on.

William had been crouching before the pipe, making a noise like a bassoon into its

interior ; but now he rose and came beam-
ingly to James. His eyes were aglow with
chumminess and affection ; and placing his
forefeet on James's chest, he licked him three
times on the face in rapid succession. And
as he did so, something seemed to snap in
James. The scales seemed to fall from
James's eyes. For the first time he saw
William as he really was, the authentic
type of dog that saves his master from a
frightful peril. A wave of emotion swept
over him.

" William ! " he muttered. " William ! "

William was making an early supper off
a half brick he had found in the road. James
stooped and patted him fondly.

" William," he whispered, " you knew
when the time had come to change the conversation, didn't you, old boy ! " He
straightened himself. " Come, William," he
said. " Another four miles and we reach
Meadowsweet Junction. Make it snappy and
we shall just catch the up express, first stop
London."

William looked up into his face and it
seemed to James that he gave a brief nod
of comprehension and approval. James

turned. Through the trees to the east he could see the red roof of Honeysuckle Cottage, lurking like some evil dragon in ambush.

Then, together, man and dog passed silently into the sunset.

That (concluded Mr. Mulliner) is the story of my distant cousin James Rodman. As to whether it is true, that, of course, is an open question. I, personally, am of opinion that it is. There is no doubt that James did go to live at Honeysuckle Cottage and, while there, underwent some experience which has left an ineradicable mark upon him. His eyes to-day have that unmistakable look which is to be seen only in the eyes of confirmed bachelors whose feet have been dragged to the very brink of the pit and who have gazed at close range into the naked face of matrimony.

And, if further proof be needed, there is William. He is now James's inseparable companion. Would any man be habitually seen in public with a dog like William unless he had some solid cause to be grateful to him,—unless they were linked together by some deep and imperishable memory? I think not. Myself, when I observe William coming along the street, I cross the road and look into a shop window till he has passed. I am not a snob, but I dare not risk my position in Society by being seen talking to that curious compound.

Nor is the precaution an unnecessary one. There is about William a shameless absence of appreciation of class distinctions which recalls the worst excesses of the French Revolution. I have seen him with these eyes chivvy a pomeranian belonging to a Baroness in her own right from near the Achilles Statue to within a few yards of the Marble Arch.

And yet James walks daily with him in Piccadilly. It is surely significant.

THE END